BURY MY
HEART

AT CONFERENCE ROOM B

THE UNBEATABLE
IMPACT OF TRULY
COMMITTED MANAGERS

STAN SLAP

BURY MY HEART

AT CONFERENCE ROOM B

PORTFOLIO PENGUIN

PORTFOLIO PENGUIN
Published by the Penguin Group
Penguin Group (USA) Inc., 375 Hudson Street,
New York, New York 10014, U.S.A.
Penguin Group (Canada), 90 Eglinton Avenue East, Suite 700,
Toronto, Ontario, Canada M4P 2Y3
(a division of Pearson Penguin Canada Inc.)
Penguin Books Ltd, 80 Strand, London WC2R 0RL, England
Penguin Ireland, 25 St. Stephen's Green, Dublin 2, Ireland
(a division of Penguin Books Ltd)
Penguin Books Australia Ltd, 250 Camberwell Road, Camberwell,
Victoria 3124, Australia
(a division of Pearson Australia Group Pty Ltd)
Penguin Books India Pvt Ltd, 11 Community Centre, Panchsheel Park,
New Delhi – 110 017, India
Penguin Group (NZ), 67 Apollo Drive, Rosedale, North Shore 0632,
New Zealand (a division of Pearson New Zealand Ltd)
Penguin Books (South Africa) (Pty) Ltd, 24 Sturdee Avenue,
Rosebank, Johannesburg 2196, South Africa

Penguin Books Ltd, Registered Offices:
80 Strand, London WC2R 0RL, England

First published in 2010 by Portfolio Penguin,
a member of Penguin Group (USA) Inc.

Paperback ISBN: 9780593853856

Bury My Heart At Conference Room B is a registered trademark of Seize the World, Inc.
DBA slap.

Page vi constitutes an extension of this copyright page.

LIBRARY OF CONGRESS CATALOGING IN PUBLICATION DATA

Slap, Stan.
  Bury my heart at conference room B : the unbeatable impact of truly committed managers /
Stan Slap.
    p. cm.
  Includes bibliographical references and index.
  ISBN 978-1-59184-324-5
1. Management. 2. Organizational effectiveness. 3. Success in business. I. Title.
HD31.S5764 2010
658.4'09—dc22

                              2010005388

Set in Filosofia
Designed by Pauline Neuwirth, Neuwirth & Associates, Inc.

147141878

Thank you, Diane.
I'll be home soon.

Take 10,000 managers from seventy countries, at various levels, in different companies and lines of business. Put them in twenty-person panic rooms for a couple of days where they can say what's really on their minds and in their hearts. What do you get? Savagely ravaged muffin trays and the absolute truth.

That's what I did with *Bury My Heart at Conference Room B* before this book was written. Amid the intensity of those sessions some statistics clamored noisily for attention. Like these:

The personal values that an overwhelming number of managers in every position in every country reported as being most important to them:

1. Family
2. Integrity

The personal values that those same managers reported as being the most under pressure to compromise in order to do their jobs successfully:

1. Family
2. Integrity

File under: Big Trouble

Let me be who I am.
And let me kick out the jams.

—MC5

CONTENTS

PART 4 GET ON WITH IT

PART 5 UNDER THE HOOD
Research proof points, notes, acknowledgments and the inevitable primate studies, Sun Tzu and Rumi quotes

A MANAGER'S DREAM

THE PATH THAT we're about to take in this book is intended to be provocative and productive for you. The first step out of the gate has to be knowing where you want to end up. What do you really want from your company?

Even if you can't put a name on it you can probably put a name on the feeling that comes from not getting it. Managers I've talked with sure have done that—in strategy sessions, in executive coaching meetings, after keynote speeches, during casual conversations and in serious interviews for this book.

Most of them want to serve and build their companies, and they want to win. But none of them wants success completely defined on their company's terms; they want it defined on their own terms, too.

● ● ●

I want to live my most important personal beliefs at work. I want to take with me to work the best of what my life gives me. I want enough personal energy left at the end of the day so the rest of my life isn't just a work-release program.

I want respect. I want to be in a position to be depended upon, but since my choice of how dependable I'm going to be is discretionary, I want it understood as the gift that it is. I want the job of manager to be appreciated as being part art and part science—modern art and forensic science. I want to be recognized for having a job that's often unrecognizable on a day-to-day basis. I want to be paid to think, not just to comply. I want to be trusted.

I want control. I want authority that matches my accountability. I want a job that's interesting and challenging but not regularly an interesting challenge to survive. I want my company to stop referring to its managers as the linchpin of the enterprise or else to start treating us like the linchpin of the enterprise. I want to know that I'm creating a dependable sanctuary with my hard work, and I want to know that the harder I work the more sanctuary I'll create. I want to trust.

I want impact. I want to know that the work I do means something to somebody and helps to make the world, if not a better place, at least not a worse one. I want to know that there's some actual lasting value to how I spend my time and that I'm contributing to something that won't always be immediately forgotten in the rush to the next urgent priority. I want a legacy. I want affiliation. I want to be in a healthy relationship, not one where it seems I'm constantly begging for love and forgiveness for mysterious sins. I want a real connection with people I spend so much time with, and I want time to help my own people realize who they can be, not just what they can do. I want to know I'm contributing to a company that can be counted on to do the right thing. I want a job that rewards my faith.

I want a reason to believe.

INTRODUCTION

I FIGURE I'M PRETTY qualified to write the introduction to this book. I've managed companies, I spent ten years developing the solution and I've beta tested it in the real and sometimes surreal world of managers for another ten.

There's only one person more qualified: A manager currently running strategy, projects, headcount and a P&L. A manager who was already very successful and fulfilled but became much more of both due directly to the unique point of view and process you'll discover in these pages.

So I asked a few of the many who've experienced *Bury My Heart at Conference Room B* to explain what it has done for them. And I asked them what they'd say to you—manager to manager—as someone who is considering it for the first time.

I'm going to let some good people talk to you now. I'll be back with you right after and we'll ramp it up.

● ● ●

■ WHEN MARK HURD, THE CEO OF HEWLETT-PACKARD, TAPS YOU, YOU'RE GOING TO FEEL IT. THREE YEARS AGO, HE APPOINTED ADRIAN JONES TO BE THE CHANNEL CHIEF FOR THE AMERICAS—25,000 COMPANIES THAT REPRESENT A MAJOR REVENUE SOURCE FOR HP. ADRIAN AGGRESSIVELY SET ABOUT TO CREATE WHAT IS NOW REC- OGNIZED AS THE SUCCESSFUL MODEL OF AN ENTERPRISE-PARTNER RELATIONSHIP. SO MR. OPPORTUNITY JUST TAPPED HIM AGAIN, THIS TIME AS AN SVP, TO TURN AROUND THE COMPANY'S JAPAN- APAC REGION, WHICH MANY BELIEVE IS THE AREA OF ITS GREAT- EST FUTURE GROWTH. ADRIAN IS SMART AND DISCIPLINED; IF HIS CAREER HISTORY IS ANY INDICATION, HE'LL GIVE THIS MASSIVE NEW JOB HIS TOTAL MIND AND BODY. OTHER THAN THE ONE SHOULDER HURD KEEPS TAPPING, WHICH HAS GONE COMPLETELY NUMB.

"My first exposure to *Bury My Heart at Conference Room B* was years ago, as a regional manager for Quantum. I thought I knew everything. Had plenty of energy even if I wasn't sure what to use it for—was a cheeky, unguided missile. I know I should have been more skeptical about the process because it seems like it makes you vulnerable. In the end it makes you so much stronger and I think I must have sensed that.

"It instantly changed my whole philosophy of managing. It showed me that you could transform people's lives in a business environment in a way they thought was impossible. Since then I've seen the metrics impact of *Bury My Heart at Conference Room B*—numbers up, better productivity, people more motivated, my team rated the best in the company and the best results in the channel space we've ever had at Hewlett-Packard. But that very first time? I was overwhelmed by the message.

"When you grow up as a manager and aspire to higher and higher levels, business culture teaches you to keep all the emotions in. You must manage people a certain way; you must accept certain things as the way things are; you should not reveal yourself. Those are the rules.

"*Bury My Heart at Conference Room B* taught me to break the rules.

"I'm a very passionate guy and what this showed me is that it really is okay to be passionate, to put your true heart into what you do. I've learned that the rest doesn't matter—who you are when you get up every morning is what matters. This is what I know now that I can pass on to you: Let the walls come down. Don't lead from your head. Lead from what you believe in."

■ RICK DEVENUTI IS A NOTORIOUSLY TOUGH MANAGER WHO WORKS BEST IN NOTORIOUSLY TOUGH ENVIRONMENTS. HE IS A FORMER CIO OF MICROSOFT, WHERE HE ALSO RAN ITS PROFESSIONAL SERVICES AND SUPPORT DIVISION, EMPLOYING 17,000 PEOPLE, AND IS NOW COO FOR EMC'S CONTENT AND ARCHIVING ORGANIZATION. THE GUY HAS ALWAYS BEEN KNOWN AS AN EXECUTION MACHINE: HARD-HEADED AND HEADED FOR RESULTS. THOSE WHO'VE WORKED FOR HIM HAVE ALWAYS SUSPECTED THAT HIDDEN UNDERNEATH ALL THAT STEEL IS . . . APPARENTLY MORE STEEL.

"I have been successful my entire career, getting a promotion every two to three years. From the beginning it was, 'This is what it takes to be successful?' Okay, because I *am* going to be successful. I thought I needed to be harsh to get results, including being harsh with myself. Nobody ever encouraged me to seek deep fulfillment for its own sake or to help drive my success, so I didn't encourage it in others. In a results-obsessed environment, thinking about the person becomes distracting. Whether you had a good weekend or not isn't relevant to my mission. Whether I had a good weekend or not isn't relevant to yours.

"I may not have liked what a hard-ass I needed to be. I mean, who wants to tell someone they'll lose their job? On the other hand, here are your costs and here are your revenues and those two numbers have to make sense one way or the other, and there are only so many ways to do that. Every manager has accountability and resources pressures, but when you get to a very senior level the deliverables and ramifications of missing them are so big, to so many different groups. Very few people at that level ever feel, 'I've made it. I can relax.' If you can't find some way to tune out the internal conflict, it will kill you.

"I'd heard great things about *Bury My Heart at Conference Room B* from successful people I respected. But it made me nervous: Was it going to open a door with my organization that I clearly did not want opened? Would it lead to an unraveling of what was very carefully, tightly wound inside of me?

"It made me look deeper at myself than almost anything in my life—as powerful as the birth of my children. The thing *Bury My Heart at Conference Room B* did for me that I've never been able to get back in the bottle is show me how compartmentalized I had made my life. There was a Work Rick, a Home Rick, a Dad Rick and a Husband Rick. I played each of those roles for a certain amount of hours a day.

"How I treated others—as numbers instead of people—I think completely differently about that now. I would have said you can show no vulnerability in your career to be successful. I've found it's just the opposite. My belief now is, when people can't see you as a person, they can't trust you. If they can't trust you, you can't lead them.

"*Bury My Heart at Conference Room B* has made me less harsh, but it isn't a softening process—it gives you real strength to be intense and focused. I'm very proud of the results I've achieved in my career, but if I'd had this twenty years earlier, I'd be a lot prouder of who I was as a person.

"What I'd want to tell any manager is that this process taught me you can only bring your best to home and work if you're being true to who you are in both places. If you don't do that, guaranteed you won't be your best in either one.

■ JANET ROLLE DANCED PROFESSIONALLY FOR FIVE YEARS, THEN PIROUETTED TO COLUMBIA BUSINESS SCHOOL, WHERE SHE ADDED AN MBA. AT MTV NETWORKS SHE WAS VICE PRESIDENT OF PROGRAM ENTERPRISES AND BUSINESS DEVELOPMENT FOR VH1 AND COUNTRY MUSIC TELEVISION. AS VP AND GENERAL MANAGER AT AOL SHE BUILT BLACK VOICES INTO THE NUMBER ONE AFRICAN AMERICAN INTERNET DESTINATION. SHE'S NOW THE CHIEF MARKETING OFFICER OF BET (BLACK ENTERTAINMENT TELEVISION), THE VIACOM DIVISION THAT'S

THE LARGEST BLACK ENTERTAINMENT COMPANY IN THE WORLD. ALL IN ALL, SOME PRETTY SWEET MOVES.

"I first experienced *Bury My Heart at Conference Room B* with my peer group, the chief officers of Black Entertainment Television. I work with these people every day in intense circumstances and we depend on one another, yet it became clear we didn't know each other in the most important way: what we each value most. Really, so much of what you do as a manager has nothing to do with what the source of your humanity actually is.

"Before this experience it hadn't really occurred to me just how much a group of successful black managers at a predominantly black company might still feel the need to subjugate ourselves in order to succeed in the larger world of business. No matter how smart and educated we are, people don't assume we're qualified. So we've been trained to suppress our passion, to closet who we are.

"*Bury My Heart at Conference Room B* humanized us to each other in ways that none of us could have anticipated. It has strengthened us.

"On a personal level, I always thought I was pretty self-aware. I had done the 360s and the psychological tests and always got high marks, but *Bury My Heart at Conference Room B* has given me a framework for understanding what had created success for me and how I could re-create it going forward. I hadn't recognized that the same values of passion, creativity and freedom that drove me in dance were driving me in business. My first thought was that this explains every good and bad decision I've ever made. My second thought was, where was this when I was twenty-one and really could have used it? Hello?

"*Bury My Heart at Conference Room B* has allowed me to make better decisions, from a results standpoint for the company, but also better in terms of my comfort with them. Now I can tell what causes me to be detached in any situation and stop it from happening. Is there any greater way of guaranteeing results?

"If there is something inside of you that is making you read this book, I would say, congratulations, because I think such a person instinctively feels the desire to do better and to be better. I congratulate you for having picked it up in the first place and want to welcome you to the club that's been enlightened by it."

■ MIKE DeCESARE IS THE ARCHETYPAL SALES MONSTER. BRED AND FED IN THE MOST INTENSE SELLING ENVIRONMENTS. SHIFTER STUCK IN FIFTH, SWEATS DETAILS OF THE DETAILS, INTUITIVELY SENSES THE POTENTIAL OF MEETING QUARTERLY TARGETS LIKE THE INDIANS USED TO SENSE DISTANT BUFFALO AND HAS A WORK HARD/PLAY HARDER STAMINA THAT IS CONTAGIOUS TO ANYONE IN THE ROOM— ANYONE IN THE ROOM THAT'S STILL STANDING. HE IS THE EXECUTIVE VICE PRESIDENT OF WORLDWIDE SALES AT McAFEE, WHERE HE RUNS A 2,500-PERSON ORGANIZATION.

"People who don't understand sales teams think they're motivated by money. They're motivated by recognition. They're not gathered in one place, they're always on the clock, every single day, and they move fast. If you want people to perform incredibly well under these conditions, they have to be massively reinforced and they have to trust you at an entirely different level. This is what *Bury My Heart at Conference Room B* does.

"I have brought it into three companies engaged in insane competitive circumstances. Without exception, there has been a direct, measurable connection between my top-performing managers and the ones who apply this process. At McAfee it was the catalyst to help slam attrition from 35 percent to 5 percent in one year. My managers constantly rate it as the most profound moment in their professional careers.

"The personal impact on me has been huge, the biggest development I've ever experienced. It's what allowed me to link my personal priorities with my work priorities. It helped me discover there are certain things I will not bend on as a human being and showed me how to design an organization that is fulfilling for me in that way. It's so integrated into my success that I can't imagine what my life and career would have been like without this. I mean, what would your life be like if you didn't have kids?

"My message to managers is that you can learn about account planning, take lessons about how to interview, get an MBA so you know how to run a P&L, but there's nothing else that prepares you for the nonoperational parts of running an organization like *Bury My Heart at Conference Room B* does.

"I'd like to think my career can stack up fairly well as being credible and rewarding, but when I found this, something changed for me, something completely different became available. What I'm saying is that there's so much useless information out there, it would be a shame to let this one get away. *Bury My Heart at Conference Room B* isn't hypothetical. This is real. This is good."

◉ ◉ ◉

In the years since I first developed this process, I've seen *Bury My Heart at Conference Room B* change the lives of many managers. Managers from executive to entry level and from Manhattan to Mumbai. These managers regularly report that the same concepts and methods included in this book were a transformational experience, rattling their bones and homesteading in their souls.

Your turn now. Buckle up: We're going off-road.

—STAN SLAP
TURKS AND CAICOS ISLANDS*

---

* Written in our San Francisco offices, but I've always wanted to say that.

The best way to do is to be.

—LAO TZU

PART 1
IT TAKES A VALUE PROPOSITION

What matters most is how well you

walk through the fire.

—CHARLES BUKOWSKI

WHAT LIES UNDERNEATH

1

THE PROBLEM SNAKES straight up the main line, clamping off vital flow to the enterprise. It is directly linked to fluctuating revenue, poor strategic execution, lack of innovation, rising compensation costs, job dissatisfaction and attrition of top talent. Larger companies feel the scale of the problem; smaller companies feel the acute threat of the problem.

This is the book about solving the problem. This is the book about achieving emotional commitment in managers.

A manager's emotional commitment is the ultimate trigger for their discretionary effort, worth more than financial, intellectual and physical commitment *combined*. It's the kind of commitment that solves unsolvable problems, creates energy when all energy has been expended and ignites emotional commitment in others, like employees, teams and customers. Emotional commitment means unchecked, unvarnished devotion to the company and its success; any legendary organizational performance is the result of emotionally committed managers.

Not everything that can be counted counts and not everything that counts can be counted, said Einstein. This is a guy who conducted early nuclear experiments on his own hair and so is perhaps not your most reliable organizational thinker; still, he had a point. The really important measurements of emotional commitment include the ones a company can't see until managers need to show them. Ferocious support for the company when the company needs it most is one of these hidden metrics.

Any manager can appear fully productive and enthusiastic simply because they're financially, intellectually and physically committed. But if you've ever witnessed a human being emotionally committed to a cause—working like they're being paid a million when they're not being paid a dime—you know there's a difference and you know it's big.

It's big, but it's not easy. The issue of gaining emotional commitment from managers is typically one of manic yet unrequited corporate lust. How can your company get it? Relax; these are only the first pages of the book—more about that later. Besides, the question isn't *how* as much as *why*. Why would any manager choose to give such a thing to their company or, more accurately, why wouldn't they? If you're a manager, you may know the answer to this question. If you don't, hang on a minute. Only. First. Pages. Of. Book.

Foreshadowing: Emotional commitment is even more important to you than it is to your company.

YOU HAD ME AT "EVEN MORE IMPORTANT TO YOU"

Ever have the uneasy feeling that no matter how rewarding your job is you're missing something? Are you suspicious that there's some still-higher level of work fulfillment available to you? Lingering in the mist, just out of reach . . . if only you could crack the code to finding it?

There is, and emotional commitment is the key to the code.

You'll gain plenty of professional benefits from your emotional commitment, including the sharpening of every management skill you already have and a rarefied ability to achieve results through others, but the biggest perks transcend the job. The key neurobiological source of emotional commitment is the ability to live your own deepest values in a relationship or environment. As a manager, this means the relationship with your company and your environment at work.

Imagine making decisions based on what you most deeply believe is the right way to live. Getting accepted and rewarded for being who you really are. Experiencing nonstop energy from constant confirmation of your true self. Feeling certain in the most uncertain of times. Displaying rock-solid consistency between your intentions and your actions—even under pressure, especially under pressure. This is what it means to live your values. Achieve all of this at work and both you and your company will be a whole lot richer for it.

It's tough to mount anything other than an insane argument *against* the value of emotional commitment. This shouldn't be a book; it should be a pamphlet.

WHY IT'S A BOOK

It never fails: Get any few managers together and they're sane and sensible about how they want to live and work, and live at work. Put a bunch of them together, some bizarre herd mentality takes over and they begin to legislate against themselves.

There is no evil brain in a jar behind the curtain. Who is it that creates, mandates and accepts violations of how managers want to live at work? *Managers*—acting as management, the honor guard of the enterprise. Focused, vigilant and unfortunately contributing to the threat, not resolving it. As if living personal values at work doesn't have anything to do with business—as if it doesn't directly affect managers' commitment and managers' commitment doesn't decide the success of the company.

And so the battle rages on over emotional commitment with no one ever declared the winner. On one side, companies seem condemned to artificial life support—the constant combination of bribing, bullying and bleating used to keep managers productive and paying attention. On the other, managers seem condemned to being materially enriched as a trade-off for ultimate fulfillment, a problem that often goes unrecognized until it's way too late to reconcile. You and your company may be successful while enduring these conditions, but for how long, at what cost and versus what potential? What definition of success?

Like most standoffs, the problem is rooted in mutual misunderstanding. As you'll learn in this book, what companies want most from their managers is what they most stop their managers from giving. What managers want most from their jobs is what they most stop themselves from getting.

You would no doubt savor this delicious irony if it didn't happen to affect you personally.

THE PRESENCE OF YOUR ABSENCE

Whoa, *whoa*. Is someone saying that you're not emotionally committed to your company? You believe in your company and brag endlessly about it. You rock around the clock, working days, nights and weekends for your company. You wear nothing but commemorative company T-shirts and might even if they weren't free. What greater love hath any manager?

Ah, but emotional commitment is a tricky thing, a delicate process that's buried far below the level of conscious choice. It will happen only when your brain believes it's safe to give it and is uniquely rewarded for giving it. The critical signal for both is if you're able to live your deepest personal values at work. As a manager, can you say that's the case—no hesitation or qualification? Careful now: Even a financially rewarding, intellectually stimulating work environment isn't the same as living your own values.

The default position for emotional commitment is emotional detachment, which manifests itself in all sorts of ways. Could you possibly be emotionally detached at work without even realizing it? It would be hard to realize if you're detached. There's a party in your head and you're not invited.

Emotional detachment can just as easily mobilize you as paralyze you, so working a lot and thinking about work a lot aren't always accurate indicators of emotional commitment to work. On the other hand, you may be able to draw a clear distinction between what happens at work and the rest of your life, but should that distinction be so easy? If you could bring the best of who you are to work, would that distinction be so necessary?

WHY IT CAN'T WAIT

I didn't write this book because I found the subject to be interesting. I wrote it because I believe it's an urgent problem to solve.

Those 10,000 managers who said they weren't living personal values of family and integrity at work? They didn't say family is being compromised because they don't spend enough time at home. They said the sure sense of community and support they received at home wasn't translating to the place they spend over half their waking hours. They didn't say integrity is being compromised because they're being forced to lie, cheat and steal for their company. They said there was a disturbingly low amount of integrity between who they really are and who they are at work.

Whenever a deep divide exists between who someone is as a human being, who they want to be as a manager and who they have to be as management, all hope for emotional commitment is lost. Lost for managers and lost for the companies that depend on them.

WHAT ARE WE TALKING ABOUT HERE?

We are talking about nothing less than redrawing the potential for organizational success. The great plains of corporate possibility are a wasteland unless deep-seeded by a wholly different level of manager commitment. Little is grown and nothing is sustainable. Companies will never change this until they change who managers can be within the company.

We are talking about nothing less than redrawing the potential for manager fulfillment. Providing the ultimate solution to work/life balance: not escaping from work but living the way you want to at work.

This is all still very new thinking. New thinking requires smart connection of seemingly unrelated empirical data points, accurate interpretation of anecdotal evidence and the occasional leap of faith.

Most of all, it requires a deep desire to live in the new rather than continue to suffer in the old.

TIME TO DEAL IN THE REAL

If we want to make things right, we've got to be up front about what's wrong. Fierce truths must be told.

Is your company a safe place to give emotional commitment? Maybe not. That doesn't mean it's a bad company with evil intent aimed directly at you; save those conspiracy theories for your next performance appraisal. But it is a company and as such it's a self-serving economic organism that cares more about its own survival and prosperity than it does about you and yours.

I can't tell you that your company will ever be that safe place. But I can show you how to make yourself safe in a possibly unsafe place. This book will show you exactly how to turn your job into a mechanism that fulfills your deepest personal values.

Your company will benefit: You'll work hard to protect that mechanism by making your company successful. And you'll benefit as a manager: You can't meet your values without the support of your employees, so this book is going to show you how to turn your values into something of urgent benefit for them. As a result, they'll work hard to protect you by making you successful.

Consider all that stuff a gift with purchase. *Bury My Heart at Conference Room B* is about gathering all available power—and power tools—to carve yourself a place of deep fulfillment at work. If you're dissatisfied with your life as a manager, this is going to make you satisfied. If you're pretty satisfied, this is going to make you more satisfied. If you're completely satisfied, that's good. A rich fantasy life is important to overall mental health.

This book isn't for those collected at the bottom of the hill. It's aimed at those who want to be the best at what they do—best at managing and best at living.

THE MYSTERY ACHIEVEMENT

2

L ET'S GET RIGHT on top of the bottom line: You must live your personal values at work. This isn't some woo-woo new paradigm management rhetoric. This is, flat out, the quality of your life.

Profitability. Growth. Quality. Exceeding customer expectations. These are not examples of values. These are examples of corporate strategies being sold to you as values. They may be good, important strategies, but they're strategies all the same. Values are different; values are deeply held personal beliefs.

Family. Integrity. Health. Freedom. These are examples of values. If these are some of your own biggest values and you feel that you have to compromise them in any way to do your job, you may not be fully living your values at work. This isn't a matter of your intelligence, maturity or skill; there are relentlessly seductive forces being aimed at you as companies attempt to replicate a sense of personal-values fulfillment for managers but insert corporate priorities in its place.

You can be a smart and sophisticated manager who has Family as a core value—and easily end up believing that you need to never see your family so you can make a bunch of money to take care of your family by killing the competition and, by extension, other people and their families, even though Harmony and Spirituality are also among your top values. And you can ignore that this is happening even though your value of Integrity, of which issues like accountability, self-awareness and congruency play key parts, is being regularly jeopardized.

Hmmm.

"Manager" can be a great job to have and you may be having a great time doing it. But embedded in any manager's job description is the requirement to regularly subordinate or compromise personal values in favor of company priorities. This doesn't mean you're out there committing vile acts as part of some Faustian bargain (even if you are, pay attention), but it does mean that what your company wants done and how it wants it done must often take precedence over your own deep preferences. This is what it means to be a manager: Serve your company first.

Emotional detachment is a logical reaction in the face of this constant struggle. Warning: Detachment only seems like a safe place. It takes far more energy to be emotionally detached than emotionally committed, to maintain a wall between your inner and outer selves. This is energy that's no longer available to put into realizing the rest of your life.

Could you choose to live without always meeting your values at work? Sure, but the problem is, life doesn't get graded on the curve. It's impossible to spend over half your waking hours ignoring, subordinating or compromising your deepest-held personal beliefs and the other half in total fulfillment of those same beliefs. There is no safe container to store your values while you're at work; not living your deepest values is going to leak on you.

Okay, so much for the first few perky paragraphs.

We're not talking rage against the machine here. The company you help manage may provide more opportunities for you and your family than you ever dreamed possible. You may love your job, be proud and endlessly fascinated by the work you do. Those are beautiful things, but it's not what this thing is all about. This is about not mistaking personal and professional fulfillment as automatically synonymous. This is about serving yourself first to better serve your company. And this is about keeping a careful eye on that chronology in the face of constant pressure to reverse it.

Being loyal to yourself doesn't have to come at the loss of being loyal to your company. You'll give up nothing to live your personal values at work. The same can't be said about choosing not to.

RENDEZVOUS WITH REALITY

You may want to give emotional commitment to your company; if you can give it, that means it's safe to give it and you want to be safe in a world you're devoting so much of your life to. But as a manager you have a lot of indications that giving it isn't such a fabulous idea. After all, every other type of commitment you've fed your company has been slurped down greedily and, my God, it's *still* hungry. Willing to work fifty hours a week? Your company will take sixty. Willing to back those strategies that are obviously brilliant? You're expected to back the ones that are obviously boneheaded with equal fervor. Willing to work hard for bonuses and options when times are good? Plan on working even harder when those are things of distant memory and fuzzy future.

You were an adult before you were a manager and any adult knows the danger of recklessly offering emotional commitment. Emotional commitment is the biggest thing a human being has to give; it's unconditional, often overruling logic or self-preservation. It doesn't matter how otherwise confident you are; emotional commitment means strolling into the spotlight, buck naked and vulnerable, anxiously muttering, "Please don't hurt me." Well, sometimes you *do* get hurt, life being life. These are the hurts that last a while, therapy being therapy.

Relationships with family, friends, lovers? Those can be agonizing enough. What can you do but live through them and determinedly fling yourself back into the mosh pit of social intercourse, knowing that to do anything less is to miss the opportunity for true fulfillment?

But to close your eyes and fall confidently into the secure bosom of your company? Uh . . . yeah. Get right back to you on that.

At one time or another, every manager has felt trapped in a vague conspiracy between idiots above them and idiots below. Many are uneasily aware that they inhabit an alien planet whose rulers consider them life forms expendable at a moment's notice. Company performance requirements are often blithely dismissive of the reality that faces managers as they attempt to do their jobs well and simultaneously protect the sense of self that's required to do their jobs well.

This is a problem for managers at every level; I regularly coach CEOs and executive teams and they voice exactly the same concerns. When you're clawing your way to the top, it's easy to cling to the illusion that everything will be figured out and fulfilling once you get there. When you get there and find that's not the case, you've gained all apparent rewards the job has to offer, everybody expects you to know everything, you can't easily admit what doesn't feel good, things still don't make sense and there's nowhere else to go. . . . People jump from the top floors of buildings, not the bottom.

I've rarely met managers who've come into their jobs with a cynical worldview, but I've met plenty who've adopted one as a protective mechanism. Yet most managers still have plenty of emotional commitment to give to their jobs if they can be convinced it makes sense to give it.

THE HOW AND WHY OF WHAT MATTERS

Which brings us to *Bury My Heart at Conference Room B.* You hold in your hands the book that will help it all make sense—that will put a lot more purpose and soul into the job of management. Along the way, it will help you do great things for your company, your people and your customers. But this is not a management book. This is a book for managers.

C-level or entry level, this is also a book for you as a human being. Sounds simple, gets complicated: As a human being, you're responsible for yourself. As a manager, you're also responsible for others. As a member of management, you're furthermore responsible for your company and for all who depend on its success. You have to wear a lot of hats, you have to wear them constantly and you have to wear them all at the same time.

Well, it's a look.

Let me help you with that look. If you're going to invest time reading a business book, you deserve to know there's a strong case for economic and organizational impact contained within it. Not a problem: Emotional commitment isn't soft stuff; it's the stuff of hard-core results. To prove it, we'll first explore the impact of securing emotional commitment from an entire management organization. I'll show you the spectacular success enjoyed by some companies who've done it and how they're able to achieve goals and resolve problems in ways unimaginable to the average company.

Are you responsible for the supervision of an entire management organization and solely concerned about its business performance? I'll prove that emotional commitment won't be a Trojan horse rolled past the company gates on your watch, spilling soldiers of the heart to seduce and corrupt staunch fiscal battalions. You'll see that it doesn't come at the cost of any other kind of manager commitment—it's an accelerant to all other kinds of management commitment. It's the mother of all other kinds of management commitment.

As I was wrapping up the writing of this book, I grabbed 750 managers' names from all the many thousands who have undergone the *Bury My Heart at Conference Room B* process for a quick written survey. I asked them to rate the impact on their performance and the drivers of that performance. No surprises in the responses from this sample:

92 percent responded that it has changed the way they do their jobs

92 percent responded that it has increased their ability to lead their people

86 percent responded that it has improved their job satisfaction

83 percent responded that it has increased the commitment of their employees

82 percent responded that it has improved their overall sense of fulfillment in life

The best corporate revenues will be achieved as a result of your managers' commitment to themselves, made before any commitment to the company. Get one Manager Commitment as a result of the other Manager Commitment and you have a powerful equation for Earnings: $E = MC^2$.

Sometimes companies get emotional commitment from their managers in the early garage days. Sometimes they get it in times of tremendous gain or pain. This book is about getting it from your managers on a sustained, self-reinforced basis.

WHERE WE'RE GOING RIGHT NOW

Bury My Heart at Conference Room B is the highest-rated management solution in a number of the world's highest-rated companies. Which is swell, and in this book we'll look at some companies that have resolved the problem of emotional commitment, but I won't waste your time with yet another report on the oft-eulogized best and brightest.

This book is a solution and that means I'm going to show you how you can get the benefits in your own company—how your company can get them—but first and more importantly, how *you* can get them. Approaching this solely from an enterprise perspective might make an impressive case study, but it won't get us very far in actual pursuit of fixing the problem. Emotional commitment is a personal choice on the part of every human being. Managers understand this even when their companies don't.

Regardless of your position, I promise I'll get you wicked smart about how this commitment happens in a human being. I'll explain why gaining it seems so difficult for even the smartest companies and the counterintuitive leap required. You'll learn why the choice to deprive your company of emotional commitment may have occurred without your even noticing it, and why it's a reasonable choice that has nothing to do with caring about the company. This understanding isn't just intended as a tripping of the epiphany lights. It will help give you energy for executing what comes next.

Next we're going to move straight to improving your fulfillment as a manager. I'll give you the step-by-step plan to gain the benefits of emotional commitment. You'll learn exactly how to sell the whole thing to your people and how to live your values at work even if you doubt your company will embrace the concept.

You won't get fired for reading this book. Fired up but not fired. If you're running the company, your managers won't quit from reading this book. They'll quit putting up with the conditions that stop them from being fulfilled, but they won't quit. This is a good thing: You *want* them to quit enduring those conditions. The heart of a company's performance is hardwired to the hearts of its managers.

TIME WAITS FOR NO MANAGER

3

"Point the problem somewhere else," you may be thinking. "I already meet my personal values. I'm an adult and in my personal life, of course, I protect and promote my personal values. But I'm also a manager and at work I protect and promote the company's values."

Such thinking is certainly reasonable. And definitely dangerous.

On average, how many hours a week do you spend working—meetings, e-mail, people problems, crazed customers, not to mention any actual work that accidentally occurs in between? Let's say, like most managers, it's about fifty.

On average, how many hours a week do you spend traveling to and from and for work? Some managers are dazed road warriors, but for most it's about ten. Now you're at sixty hours a week: You're working fifty and traveling ten.

On average, how many hours a week do you spend thinking about work? Not actually engaged in doing the job but obsessing about the job, talking to someone outside the job about the job, daydreaming about the job and waking up screaming about the job? If you're like most managers, it's about fifteen hours a week. Now you're at seventy-five hours a week: You're working fifty, traveling for work ten and thinking about work fifteen.

At seventy-five hours a week, you're spending more than double your waking hours working than not working.[*]

Welcome to your personal life.

What? You're thinking you get these hours back when Death sends you an e-mail?

This is it.

These are the irretrievable hours of your personal life—you do not get this time back. And if, like most managers, you're spending an average of seventy-five hours a week between work time, travel time and think time, you're spending far more of your waking hours working than not working. Every day. Every week. Every month. Every quarter. Every project. Every year.

To not live your deepest personal values for over half your waking hours is a crime. Worse, it's an unnecessary crime. Your company might actually *insist* you live them at work. You just have to know how to make this happen.

---

[*] Trying to find a flaw in the math? Here goes and good luck: Figure you're awake for sixteen hours of each day. 16 hours x 7 days = 112 hours. Seventy-five of those hours are working, which means thirty-seven are not. Seventy-five is 202.7 percent of thirty-seven. Make sense? Maybe mathematically.

The day is coming when a single carrot,

freshly observed, will set off a revolution.

—PAUL CÉZANNE

PART 2
WALLET. HEART.
KEYS.

The revolution will not be televised.

The revolution will be live.

—GIL SCOTT-HERON

THE COMPANY DREAM 4

W HAT DOES A company want from its managers? It wants you to be fanatically loyal, ferociously energized, protective of the organization and its assets, willing to represent the company as immaculate in its offerings and innocent in its intentions, flexible but consistent, innovative but obedient, bold but conservative, diverse but similar, self-sufficient but a team player, firm and sharp but soft and pliable, dependably motivated by money but independently wealthy to the point where company compensation is a personal accounting bother and not worth collecting.

A company mostly wants homeostasis—it wants to be a stable and self-structuring organization. Sexy engineering talk: A homeostatic system adapts itself to its environment to preserve stability. The system is constantly energized and will rapidly respond not only to manual changes but also to any unexpected conditions. All critical variables are held at a desirable level by a self-regulatory mechanism.

In a corporate homeostatic system, self-regulating mechanisms (that would be you) would know what to do when the system isn't productive or profitable enough and be instantly responsive. You'd act in support of the larger system and consider your function to be that and nothing more; no higher order of fulfillment would be necessary.

But wait: A company doesn't just want its managers to be hordes of Zegna-clad thermostats, reactive to any change in the business climate that could adversely affect the enterprise. It dreams big. It wants you to be proactive, anticipating those changes and transforming them into opportunities. It wants you to pursue growing the business like a holy crusade. It wants you to *care*.

It wants you to be emotionally committed.

And no wonder: The results of emotional commitment are drool-inspiring. You know them all: The groovy Internet company, the feisty regional airline, the high-minded clothing manufacturer, the zany retailer. These are places where the *weird stuff* happens all the time—the remarkable acts of manager dedication that compel success against the market, against the competition and sometimes against all odds. Emotionally committed managers in these companies don't always make the most money, but they don't leave. They champion their companies and if the EBIT hits the fan, they protect the company at all costs.

A TALE OF
TWO COMPANIES

5

PRIDE Industries

PRIDE Industries earned its entrepreneurial street cred in righteous fashion: Started in the basement of a church, it recently nailed annual revenues of over $150 million. An outsourcing solutions company, PRIDE serves manufacturing and service industries across eleven states. It's headquartered in Sacramento, California, and has notched honors as the fastest-growing company in the state capital by revenue nine years in a row. It's ISO-certified and the winner of a bunch of supplier awards, including one from Intel where, measured on quality, efficiency, cost reduction and safety, it beat 7,000 other companies and became one of three service firms ever to achieve such recognition.

PRIDE is one of the largest employers of people with disabilities in the United States.

■ ■ ■

"We're damn well not a charitable act for our customers," bristles CEO Michael Ziegler. "We're in a regular cutthroat, hypercompetitive business. We'd never make the mistake of thinking it's anything else and neither would they."

Those customers include the likes of Hewlett-Packard. PRIDE handles all ink-jet printer supply fulfillment for HP in North and Central America and is the worldwide supplier of their repair kits. The business is regularly audited and awarded on competitive cofactors of cost and competency. "We blow their minds," grins Tim Yamauchi, PRIDE's CFO.

"This is one nonprofit company that funds its own growth," says Ziegler. "We went from 90 percent of revenues coming from the government to not a dime coming from the government. We did it because our managers work really hard and their people work really hard for them."

A PRIDE kind of story: The company was recently in hot pursuit of a huge piece of business, up for bid against a dug-in competitor. It was an idea that Ziegler insisted to all was "incredibly stupid." He pauses. "Thankfully our managers were empowered to do it anyway, since they went ahead and won the business." Even after PRIDE gained initial bid approval, the incumbent fought back hard, in every way possible. PRIDE matched them step for step and prevailed, but the fight put the company dangerously behind. Managers ended up with only five days to source custom trucks, align IT systems, form new work teams, train people and be fully operational. "Got it done," Ziegler says with an ostentatious yawn.

There are a lot of unusual things about PRIDE, but most of them have nothing to do with the disabilities of their workforce; they have to do with the way the workforce is managed. Ziegler insists that a human resources executive be authoritatively involved in every strategic decision, that PRIDE offer employees full benefits and above-market rates for even the lowest-level jobs, that employees receive monthly handwritten notes from the CEO for exceptional performance and that PRIDE always find a job for anyone who is able to perform some task.

Ziegler performs his own task spectacularly well, as a manager and particularly as a leader. He reeks of charisma and is a gruff, loud and loving presence throughout the company. He pretends outrageous offense when I accuse him at one point of being coquettish and pages people into his office, bellowing, "Am I coquettish? Answer 'No' truthfully if you want to keep your jobs!" he demands, glowering at several managers who grinningly ignore him and wander back to their offices.

"I ran profitable companies before PRIDE and so did many managers on our senior team," he points out. "I ran them the same way with the same beliefs, and they were successful. By and large, corporations have lost their soul," he insists, ramping quickly to full-fire mode. "They hide behind the almighty bottom line, but you can achieve that bottom line and still be a responsible company—responsible to the communities you operate in and for.

"In a competitive market, the case is always made that a company has no choice but to become fundamentally inhuman. This is total fiction," he argues. "You can drive the cost of whatever you're doing down, you can get a great return and you can actually be a good company. This is the stuff I think about all the time."

"Keeps you up at night?" I ask.

"I sleep just fine," he says.

PRIDE is the first nonprofit organization ever asked to become a mentor in the Small Business Administration's protégé program. How do managers make decisions in the company? "If you find out, tell me," says Ziegler. "Managers have a lot of latitude here, except about having a passion for how we do business." He is emphatic that "passion has to come from inside of our managers—I can encourage it and I do that relentlessly. I can model it and with all humility I have to say I do that very well. But it's all about finding your own passion in what you want to do with your life and connecting it to what you do with your work life.

"I want that passion for the company and I also want it for our managers as human beings—I want dignity for each of them. Let people be themselves and we'll deal with any problems that come from it. Turns out that's not a problem, and even if it were, believe me, we deal with bigger problems every day."

■　■　■

The urgency to remain vigilantly human is obvious given the profound conditions of the PRIDE workforce, but only 2,700 of the 4,300 employees are disabled. One of them is an operations manager who tells me, "I don't think about my handicap much. 'Handicapped' would mean not being allowed to be who I want to be at work. I never feel handicapped here. Write that down, please."

Rhino Records

If a group of graduate students, savvy investors or (more likely) a secret government agency set out to deconstruct rock and roll, to pursue its genome annotation and identify the source of its strange power, what would they find?

The fire down below; rabid respect for roots; reckless pursuit of passion; belief in living however you want to live and saying whatever you want to say; admittedly wretched excess; loony humor; color blindness; deliberate defiance of the establishment; a perspective about money that veers between avid interest and sneering contempt; complete obsession about some things and complete ignorance and indifference about others; less than technical competence initially but native skill and devotion that results in astonishing improvement in a few short years; a compelling vision combining 4/4-beat simple with operatically, ludicrously grandiose; an identification with the audience—not just empathetic to them but one with them. For those making the music, a feeling of being incredibly lucky to be paid for doing it. For those listening to the music, the visceral sensation of their own restless, searching spirit breaking through the chest wall only to be surrounded by others experiencing the same thing. An overnight sensation after enduring years of near starvation and blistered fingers. And no matter how many individual stars emerge, most of the best work happening as a band.

If this DNA were used to build a corporate culture, it would look like Rhino Records.

■　■　■

Born in the back of a Los Angeles record store, spunky, funky Rhino grew up amidst a record industry that had become increasingly moribund in its prioritization of money over the meaning of music. Yet Rhino refused to surrender its unique lunatic spirit and still ended up setting the enduring standard for the archiving of rock recordings in scope, sound quality and packaging. How did a company whose own managers cheerfully admitted their professional immaturity in an industry dominated by seasoned conglomerates, and that struggled to break $100,000 annually in the early years, ever survive, let alone ultimately hit $100 million annually?

This is how, according to those who were there.

"Most record companies saw a business opportunity. We were fans, first and foremost—we saw a music opportunity," says Richard Foos, who was one of Rhino's founders and its president. "Music is a great source of strength and a great distraction," agrees Harold Bronson, Rhino's other founder and its managing director. "The music moved me."

Gary Stewart was one of Rhino's first employees and rose to the critical post of senior vice president of A&R. He likens the company to punk rock, which spurned the corporatization of music in an attempt to return to the spirit of the garage. "Like every great movement, Rhino was rooted in two things: a rejection of what is happening at the time and a reclamation of what has been lost that is looking to be regained."

"As a kid, I was a record junkie with no money," recalls Foos. "I couldn't wait until my favorite group had a greatest-hits record. But I felt in my bones that the record companies really didn't know the groups—they didn't even like the groups. If you look at the first Who album—an incredibly rebellious band at the time, singing about *My Generation* and smashing guitars on stage in 1965—the back cover said, "If you enjoyed this album you're sure to enjoy the Mantovani Orchestra and *The Romantic Strings of André Kostelanetz*. It was worse than ignorance; it was disdain. It was in the wrong hands.

"I was a hippie in the '60s. Rock and roll motivated me as music and as a counterculture lifestyle—I didn't separate one from the other. The Rhino product was about protecting the music. The Rhino business was about protecting the lifestyle. I believe we are all one people, that people are equal and that they deserve freedom to do their own thing. People will rise to the cause if the cause is worth getting up for. That's what happened at Rhino."

■　■　■

"We started the company with the most unprofessional group of managers imaginable," laughs Foos.

"We were ignorant in a wonderful way," explains Stewart. "We were all flying blind but we could see the importance of what we were doing. I still can't believe some of the things they let me do. But while they indulged my personal values, it wasn't an indulgent place. We were an intensely committed management team under constant pressure to perform."

"Harold and I were young and single. We could take small salaries and live for the music. That's rock and roll. It made sense to us," says Foos.

"But we always spent money on the music," counters Bronson. "From time to time we put out stuff that we were passionate about when there was a high probability we wouldn't get any return at all. We didn't play by the rules, we took chances and we cut corners, but we never cut our integrity. You have to have your priorities set to spend your own money releasing a reissue of a band that didn't sell in the first place."

"If we knew what we were doing, we would have gotten it wrong," offers Stewart. "We did it the only way we knew, The Rhino Way."

For its managers The Rhino Way included an innovative MBO program that assigned quarterly bonuses for pursuit of a manager's personal growth, constant participation by managers in decisions from strategic direction to cafeteria menus, an annual paid week off for each manager to help their favorite charity and records that were certain to be nonsellers but were released if an individual manager believed strongly in the artist.

The Rhino Way also meant staying distinctively Rhino: Amongst their carefully annotated early releases spanning doo-wop, surf music, Latino rock, Jamaican ska and New Orleans rhythm and blues was . . . *Legends of the Accordion*, which was exactly what it appeared to be to the thirty or so people that hungered for its release and which the company advertised as, "Rhino Records presents *Legends of the Accordion* and twelve other releases to help pay for it." "So many people separate themselves in business," says Foos. "They think you have to throw your passion away—you have to be 'serious' to be successful. I never believed that was true. I think you just have to be very committed. So that's what I tried to put into the company—the ability of our managers to be themselves. I kept urging them to integrate their sides. 'Come to work and be whoever you are. I want to see more of every side, not just whatever you consider the business side.'"

Chris Tobey was Rhino's senior vice president of marketing: "Just because a manager in one company was wearing a suit and someone in our company was wearing shorts and a fez doesn't mean we weren't as on top of our own business. You look at some of the stuff we did and you'd think basket case, not case study. Yet Rhino managers cared about Rhino in a way I've only heard happens in the very best organizations."

Which is why the company kept growing, albeit at a momentum-defying crawl. They were a record company that didn't have hits in an industry that feeds on them like a coal furnace. They didn't have the big sales and they didn't get the big respect. Rhino managers built the business one loving brick at a time, keeping it moving, keeping it alive.

Then in the early '90s Rhino took a sudden turn for the best as baby boomers starting buying CDs to replace their old album collections— from thousands of new full catalog record stores that were competing for business by claiming the widest selections. "And there we were with this giant catalog we had lovingly built for fifteen years," recalls Foos delightedly. Even better, Warner Music Group acquired part of the now-credible Rhino in 1992 and licensed it to be the official archiving arm for Atlantic Records, the most legendary back catalog in the history of recorded music. (Rhino's first release was a leather-bound double CD promotional sampler. The front cover read, *The Atlantic Remasters: It's as Though We Were Taking Care of Our Best Friend's Children*.) The company started to make real money at last.

"Richard and Harold wanted to make money but only in the way they knew how," insists Stewart. "They took what they loved about music and manifested that in how they allowed us to run the company. Everybody who was passionate about something could do something about it—if you were driven you could keep on driving. I used to say, 'In another company, in another room, I think somebody is being fired for this.'

"We didn't want anything to happen to the company because it was so special. We held the belief that music could play a role in how you live your life. Managers drawn to the company had already found their personal values expressed in music and now they could bring those values with them. This was a belief system worth protecting. Rhino was a lightning rod for people who cared."

■　■　■

The entire company was ultimately bought by Warner Music Group and the building team has left, but, looking back at the original successful avatar, Foos sums it up as, "We were in the right place at the right time with the right heart."

A rock and roll heart.

WELL, SURE, BUT . . .

. . . those are special *small* companies. They're still fired by entrepreneurial energy; the original passion of the company forms the reason for being; visionary, charismatic leadership is still in place; and a clear common cause unites all managers.

As a company grows beyond this early stage, the focus shifts to an emphasis on control and consistency. A premium is placed on the predictable; it's still desirable to have this fabulous individual discretionary effort from managers, but it's a whole lot *more* desirable to have a dependable organization that reliably coordinates diverse lines of business and geographies.

You don't get the same kind of emotional commitment when a management population is in the hundreds or thousands, obsessed with complex operations and ever-increasing revenue demands. The wonderful, weird stuff just can't happen anymore.

Except in places like these . . .

A TALE OF TWO MORE COMPANIES

Quad/Graphics

At over $2 billion in annual revenues, Sussex, Wisconsin–based Quad/Graphics is the largest privately owned printing company in the Western hemisphere. In nine hangar-sized plants, Quad's massive presses thunder twenty-four hours a day, seven days a week, spinning out over a million pages between sunrises.

The company shuts down for only two reasons: fire and singing.

■   ■   ■

On July 5, 2002, the company lost Lomira, its primary storage facility, housing twenty days' worth and *fifty million* pounds of finished production. The fire that swallowed an entire ten-story building started at 9:30 on a Friday night. By midnight, Quad's managers had redirected work to every other plant in a frantic but coordinated effort to remain on schedule. By 7:00 the next morning they had a 98 percent accurate inventory of lost product. By Saturday night at 6:30 reprinting had been successfully reallocated to other plants, tons of specialty paper and ink reordered, every project rescheduled and managers had talked directly to every client potentially impacted by the disaster—thirty-nine hours after the first alarm, operations were completely restarted. Quad managers had never drilled for such an emergency.

Singing. Managers drill for the singing all year, but it doesn't help. Quad Christmas parties are extensive affairs, culminating in the entire company halting to witness the annual taking of the stage by senior managers, who perform a full musical production for the vast amusement of the employee and general management populations. It may not be a *talent* show by any reasonable definition, but it's a show of commitment and gratitude to the people of Quad. Executives get up to sort of sing and dance but only to sort of make fools of themselves. "There are a lot of ways to make a fool out of yourself in a manager position," asserts Tom Quadracci, Quad's chairman and CEO. "This isn't one of them."

Quad/Graphics was conceived in 1971 as a reaction to the massive strike at the W. A. Krueger Company, the large commercial printer where Quad founder Harry Quadracci served as a vice president. The strike embittered longtime friends and coworkers and it galvanized Harry. Tom Quadracci explains, "To understand how Quad works today, it's important to understand that a cataclysmic event started our company, one that had a lasting impression on the people who first created it."

From amongst those picketing, being picketed and crossing the picket line, people gathered and followed Harry out the door, toward the promise of something better. From the beginning, he insisted that Quad be a company that was "built by the employees, for the employees." Harry Quadracci was committed to creating an organization where individuals would be treated with respect and trust.

Ah, Harry. What do you say about a chief executive who institutes Spring Fling, a Quad tradition since 1974, where managers play hooky for the day and let employees run the entire company? Who throws a champagne party and awards a medal to the manager of a project that, after three years and a million dollars . . . didn't work? Who claims, in a 1984 President's Letter, that "clowns are a perfect symbol of the Quad philosophy of management because . . . they retain their childlike ability to be surprised"—and that year makes his entrance to the company Christmas party on an elephant? Who titles his own management philosophy MPYPIDK, meaning, "My Plan, Your Plan, I Don't Know (let's just see what happens)"? Who urges his managers to be "Killer Bees in a Bonkers World"? Who believes, "How do we develop trust? We party"?

This decidedly odd style of corporate leadership is possible only if it inspires the kind of management stewardship that ensures a tightly run, high-quality, profitable enterprise. For that response to occur throughout management ranks, Harry Quadracci would have to be someone who comes from a real place, a place of the soul and of the heart. Someone who provably trusts people, celebrates them and above all believes that "individualism is a birthright that should never be demanded by a company or sacrificed for a company."

Which is why the Lomira fire is considered by every Quad/Graphics manager to be the *good* news about July 2002. At 3:15 p.m. on the thirteenth day of that same month, word ripped through the company that an emergency Pewaukee police crew had just pulled Harry's lifeless body from the lake near his home where he had accidentally drowned.

The company had now lost something far bigger than fifty million pounds of production; it had lost its primary driving spirit. Classic destruct axiom: Lose the leader and the force behind him will surrender in chaos. Quad managers weren't sure how they were going to carry on without Harry, but one thing was never in doubt: They were going to carry on *for* Harry.

"It gets harder when you are a multibillion-dollar company, but we still do a lot of things as we've always done them," says Tom Quadracci today. "We still talk to people a lot about egalitarianism and assumed responsibility. We are still obsessed about how to make them feel important in their jobs, reward them other than with just cash and move them on to 'be'—a term that we use with our managers all the time—move them to feeling that they've become more than they ever hoped to be. We try to walk the talk in terms of our value system, which is about protecting our managers' individual value systems.

"At Quad, a manager's style has to fit them individually. It has to fit their own value structure, what their belief system is, how they relate to people—there is no right way or wrong way. We teach them, train them constantly, but not about that," Tom asserts. "Quad has kind of a

New Manager University, where I talk about my expectations for them as managers. We don't want you to play office here; we want you to work at being human."

Vice President of Finance John Fowler agrees. "Our managers are expected to adjust their schedules to get the work done and are equally expected to adjust their work schedule to live their lives, take care of what's important to them outside of the job. Do we have the competition trying to pick off our management team? Oh, yeah, I think anyone could probably double their salary at a competitive company. But it doesn't happen. Our managers don't leave."

Every manager I met with at Quad/Graphics—plenty of them, at all levels, disciplines and tenures—confirmed this. "I love my children and I love to be with them more than not being with them," declares Sherry Jasinski, customer service manager. "I love this company the same way."

Some at Quad are homegrown and know the regular world of management naught but by travelers' tales, but most have experience in other companies. Pamela Lopez, director of IT systems, explains, "If you're used to goals and objectives and constant measurements of your performance, you'll be . . . I guess 'confused' would be the word. Usually companies where you don't get a lot of feedback and tools but have severe performance requirements are pretty mean places—make it or fail. But this is the opposite. Those things are missing here because it's a supportive, trusting culture."

"Anything else missing?" I ask her.

"Budgets, for one thing," she says. "There's really only a loose budget, which means you teach people to do what's right because it's right, not because it costs a lot or it's going to cost too much."

"A manager at Quad does not have an *operating budget?*" I confirm, checking to see that the backup recorder is working.

"Correct," she says. "With that kind of open checkbook comes the responsibility of doing the right thing," she adds. "If you have a lot of rope, you'd better be good or you're going to hang yourself. It's not for every manager; this is an environment where you're going to be evaluated by the sincerity of your actions.

"Manager performance isn't measured in any traditional way at Quad and neither is the way we evaluate our people," she continues. "Managers are taught here that we don't need a golden wand in our hands to make things happen. We just need to be kind to people, teach them the way, and they will follow if it's the right way. Our employees are given performance reviews, but how it's done is totally open to individual manager design."

"You could use interpretive jazz dance if that was your thing," I joke, but she seriously considers the question.

"You know, you really could," she decides. "Harry would have loved that."

■　　■　　■

"Would Harry be proud of us? I think he would," answers Joel Quadracci, president and chief operating officer. "We've come through some very tough times in this company," concludes brother Tom. "I'm grateful for how our managers have stood together to protect us. And I thank my lucky stars that our competitors' cultures are the way they are."

SAS

All Soup Must First Pass Through the Cashier, states a sign in the SAS employee cafeteria. Beyond the disturbing biological implications, this is a telling metaphor for the culture of a company remarkably free from restrictive hierarchy. SAS sells innovative business intelligence and operates its own business intelligently too.

Over $2 billion in annual sales makes SAS the world's largest privately held software company. They've achieved thirty-three years of uninterrupted revenue growth, their clients include 92 percent of the Fortune 100 and their product is actively deployed at over 45,000 sites. You'd think this performance, especially amidst the turbulence of the IT industry, would be what gains them a revered reputation, but mention the company to other managers who've even vaguely heard of it and positive reaction is more likely because of their reputation as . . . *Heaven.* SAS gets routinely profiled for its legendary thirty-five-hour workweek; the massive corporate campus with its topflight day care, health care and soccer fields; and, of course, the tons of M&M's the company thoughtfully provides employees at no cost.

Last year they had 23 job vacancies. They received 23,760 applications.

Heaven is located in Cary, North Carolina, and in the age of the corporate campus as Roach Motel—managers check in and hopefully never check out—it's indeed refreshing to visit the original, built from the heart by founder and CEO Jim Goodnight. "Trust people, give them a good place to work, expect a lot out of them and they'll do the right thing," he maintains.

The SAS folks my researchers talk to are very nice, but after months of protracted scheduling negotiations it's clear this much-feted company is not all that interested in meeting with me about *Bury My Heart at Conference Room B.* Until I tell them that I don't want to talk about their campus—I don't care if we meet in a parking lot down the road from the campus. I want to go far beyond tangible things and instead explore the SAS ethic that drives decisions about which managers are allowed to be at work. I'm not even as interested in talking to Goodnight as in talking to his managers about what it all really means to them. There is a brief pause and the Pearly Gates swing open. . . .

■ ■ ■

"M&M's are great," protests Stu Nisbet, an SAS senior research and development director. "Corporate day care and health care are really great. But this is a *company*. We have *customers.* It's a *job.* On the other hand, it's the best job in the world and unlike any I've ever heard of.

"We don't work a thirty-five-hour workweek as has been reported," he insists. "You don't build and operate a successful, competitive company that way. But a manager here can drop the kids off at school at 7:30, work until lunch, go over to the gym, work until 5:30–6:00, have dinner with their family, log on from home and go to bed at 11:00. There's flexibility to do the work however you want to do it, through the filter of what you personally believe to be the best way to do it. It's a person-to-person relationship. There is a lot of tolerance here for trying something, for speaking your mind, for taking the unpopular point of view. You're treated like an individual, like an adult.

"We've had some tough times," he asserts, as if such a thing were a competitive accomplishment for the company that he's pleading to have acknowledged. "One year we cut profit sharing from 15 percent to 5 percent because the margins weren't there. Our down times are nothing like the real world, though, because there is a huge reserve of loyalty in this company; we have less than 4 percent turnover in our management ranks."

There's a lot of talk about what SAS does for managers compared with the typical enterprise, but it's just as instructive to look at what they don't do. Talking with managers throughout the company, and investigating the policies and systems they work under, gets you mind-gnawing data points and this kind of commentary:

- No big money—"A manager could make a lot more money at every one of our competitors."
- No performance reviews, organizational health reviews or other formal manager evaluation systems—"It happens every day in real conversations."
- No restrictive covenants—"We protect our intellectual property but your head belongs to you."
- No sudden reductions in force—"If you're a brutal manager, yeah, we'll fire you, but we'd like to think we're going to give you an opportunity to improve first. We want to salvage you, not hurt you."
- No rock star treatment, even for top technology or revenue producers—"If you want to swagger around the place like you own it, you're in the wrong place. The focus is always on what your team did, what the company did, what you did for our customers."
- No sick leave limits—"We average only 2.35 sick days used per employee per year."
- No endless meetings—"Dr. Goodnight hates meetings, just hates 'em."
- No endless bureaucratic layers preventing autonomous action— "Anybody with a good idea can usually run with it. Even if we don't think it'll work, we may support it to see what we can learn."

"We make decisions based on people rather than based on prescriptive business philosophy," one of their senior managers tells me. She smiles broadly. "We're kind of screwed up but we've been successful doing it that way.

"I was at a meeting of human resources vice presidents in Florida last week," she continues. "It came up among these other companies a lot bigger than us: 'Hey, what are you guys doing about this religious rights stuff?'

"What do you mean, 'the religious rights stuff'?" I asked them.

"Well, you know, it means people want to get together and have Bible studies."

"Oh, *that*. We've been doing that for fifteen years."

"SAS isn't worried about the, you know, the civil liberties?"

"What civil liberties? If we get enough employees that want to do it, go do it. We'll give you time; we'll give you Web space. Go pursue it if that's what makes you happy. We won't allow people to take offensive positions in the workplace, but other than that, we don't care if you have a Christian group, a Muslim group, a Hindu group—this is what allows people to be themselves at work."

She rolls her eyes recalling the panicked reactions. "I'm dumbfounded why other companies are struggling with this stuff. What do you think *happens* when you say to someone they can't do that?

"Sure, I want more money, just like anybody else," she says. "I'd rather not work. I'd rather have the $20 million. But the worst thing you can do as a manager here is to not be yourself. It's not a bad place to come to work every day."

"It wouldn't matter how hard it ever got here," Stu Nisbet declares as we wrap up. "I'm sticking with SAS because they stuck with me when I was going through some difficult times. They had faith in me. My values live here and I treat this place like my home."

■ ■ ■

And those legendary M&M's? Prowling around the campus, I finally found some on a counter in the back of one coffee room, in a quarter-filled plastic container marked *Grapefruit Wedges. Keep Refrigerated.*

WELL, SURE, BUT . . .

. . . those are special *big* companies with plenty of resources and the finest management teams money can buy. They're the best in the world at what they do, and they can afford to provide the tools that inspire emotional commitment.

What about the rest of the companies—most companies? Where the culture isn't ideal, the leadership isn't legendary, the product isn't unique and the market share isn't biggest? What about all of those quiet companies which continue to admirably plug away at the daily task of doing business, never dreaming of being on the leading edge, content only to stay *off* the ledge? Can emotional commitment happen in any company, big or small, growing or stable, innovative or traditional, good, bad or ugly?

And who cares? The important question is, can it happen in your company?

Yes, and it already does. Companies want to know how to be as big and profitable as possible, so they want to know how other companies got so big and profitable. Those case studies are fascinating, but they aren't always easy to translate from company to company. In this case, conditions most relevant to your own company are the most important. Better to look inward: Chances are, measurable examples of emotional commitment are already happening somewhere in your organization. If it's already happening, it's going to be easier to incubate and scale.

Your company may have already felt the impact of emotional commitment without recognizing it for what it was. Think about a legendary manager in the company—you may be one, O revered reader, or you may know one. This is a manager who time and again gets tossed into the worst situations, lands on their hind legs and rapidly creates success. Someone who embraces change and brings resolution to chronic problems. Who creates trust and higher purpose amongst their people and gets unparalleled levels of support for common goals. Who accepts accountability and works autonomously.

No sudden moves: You're looking emotional commitment right in the eye.

This is a manager who makes no distinction between their personal values and the values they bring to work. As a result, this is a manager who doesn't need the corporate engine to give them power. They aren't contrary to the company's spirit rallies but they may be indifferent, for this is a manager who isn't connected to the organization as much as connected to their own self.

How many times has your company forlornly wished for a whole herd of these managers—or at least two for breeding stock? Money's no good here. A company can't buy true emotional commitment from managers no matter how much it's willing to spend; this is something too valuable to have a price tag. And yet a company can't afford not to have it.

If your company wants the rest of its managers to perform like its best managers perform, then the company has to respect what makes those best managers willing to give emotional commitment. Enforcing or reinforcing it isn't as important as getting out of the way and *letting it happen*. The only way to generate dependable emotional commitment is to allow it to be self-generated. That's where it comes from.

Sounds simple, eh? Then why is this still high on the list of corporate dreams unfulfilled?

THE DREAM DENIED

6

Do COMPANIES FEEL the pain of not having emotional commitment from their managers? They feel the pain. Ask any company at any time about their top ten chronic challenges. Manager performance will always appear on the list—finding them, keeping them, paying them, training them and motivating them.

Missed deadlines, lack of innovation, fluctuating product quality and legal liability are all part of the high cost of low management commitment. That's when they *stay*. When sales managers leave, they take great customers with them; when engineering managers leave, they take great ideas with them; when charismatic managers leave, they take great people with them. How many companies can say this problem doesn't matter? How many companies can say they've put this chronic challenge behind them?

Why then has such an obvious problem not been mated with the resources and resolve to fix it? After all, the best companies are used to facing complex problems with no apparent solution in sight. When beset with a crisis, they marshal every resource, review every methodology, import and apply the best advice, focus obsessively on innovative solutions—and *solve the problem*.

From Skunk Works to Saturn to Six Sigma to one *60 Minutes* segment after another, there have always been examples of companies that have charted unusual success and lip-smackingly enjoyed the results. Everybody else in the business world knows about these examples, talks about them, covets them—and generally avoids implementing them.

Companies are driven by executive teams, most often a group of highly intelligent, highly skilled and highly compensated people, all focused on the goal of keeping the enterprise growing and profitable. They're hardly asleep at the wheel; these are people who are sometimes awake twenty-four hours a day, agonizing about whether their picture will ultimately grace the cover of *Business Week* or *Mortuary Management*. Their companies solve problems and survive or they don't solve problems and fail, and either way the people running them become smarter and better able to anticipate and resolve challenges they've faced before. This is the evolving history of business.

So where is the evolved methodology for creating the highest level of self-sustaining motivation from their manager culture? Where is the genetic corporate memory for solving this problem, subscribed to by any company without conscious thought? Why hasn't a pro forma method—the classic corporate manual—been developed for how to get the most out of managers by gaining their emotional commitment? If companies applied the same clear and courageous thinking to other critical moments in corporate evolution, we'd still be grunting in the dirt, puzzling over applications for a square wheel.

Without emotional commitment from managers a company can't ever realize the dream of being a self-structuring, self-protective system. Problems never fully stop, opportunities are never fully leveraged and, even on the best days with the biggest wins, the executive team is a little on edge amongst itself about confidently predicting the future. The company remains constantly vulnerable and expends tremendous resources, even in a mature state, focused on survival.

And yet, companies have seemingly missed fixing the one thing that threatens all other things. It just doesn't make sense.

Or does it?

FEAR ITSELF

"Organization" comes from the same root word as "organism"—and for good reason. A company *is* an organism, a self-sustaining ecosystem. Like any organism, its primary priority is to survive. In order for a corporate organism to survive, it needs managers to help it function and grow. And it needs those managers to place company priorities over personal priorities whenever necessary, to marginalize their own values and beliefs in favor of company goals and methods.

To ensure this happens, companies bribe, bluff and bully their managers. In return, companies get financial, intellectual and physical commitment. But they don't get emotional commitment, which is what they really need to ensure ultimate survival.

Companies can't get emotional commitment from their managers because the company believes it needs to be the dominant organism in the relationship, which causes managers to have to repress their own values—and so causes them to detach emotionally from their jobs. In order to really get that emotional commitment, a company would have to reattach managers to their own deep drivers—allow them to live their own values and act according to their own personal codes.

Uh, who's got the folder marked *Plan B*?

This has Company Nightmare stamped all over it. If managers were allowed to live their value of Family, maybe they wouldn't work fifty hours a week, stay away from home constantly or constantly take the job home with them. If managers were allowed to live their value of Integrity, maybe they wouldn't represent a product to customers as performing the best and at the lowest cost when it doesn't, it isn't—or it doesn't even exist yet. If managers were allowed to live their value of

Health, maybe they would resist conditions of constant stress. If managers were allowed to live their value of Freedom, maybe they would demand autonomy in decisions and pay less respect to an enforced hierarchy. If managers were allowed to live their value of Creativity, maybe they wouldn't necessarily conform to established policy.

This is the great fear of the corporate organism: If I set you free to pursue your own priorities, you'll leave me and I'll die. The problem is, managers are already free. They're free to detach, which is about as free as one can get. The company may have captured their minds, their bodies and their pockets, but that doesn't mean it's captured their hearts. Those hearts are hidden away, in a safe place. Those hearts are the source of emotional commitment.

What every manager in every company has in common is that they are human. When that humanity is denied by an anxious corporate organism, things get strange. No one acts naturally. No one feels safe or trusts anyone else. People detach to protect themselves. And no one emotionally commits.

Can companies really suffer this problem? It is perilously flawed logic to think that a company can achieve dependable success by causing managers to place their own priority beliefs in less than a priority position. When detachment is introduced into a management organization and pressure is added by insisting those managers be united and devoted, the result is instability at a foundational level. Core: Meltdown.

Even if they can't put the organizational finger on it, companies can sense the difference between emotional commitment and lesser kinds. They understand that something big is being left off the table—the gap between what their managers are giving and what they could be giving—and they attempt to close the gap.

The first attempt is to repurpose values by swapping individual definitions for corporate ones. You have Family as a value? That's beautiful. This is your family right here. Now protect it by making your numbers.

The second attempt is the selling of the emotional company store: plenty of support for a common point of view; clearly defined enemies; ever-changing rewards and punishment; constant drama and numbingly urgent pace; *über* support rallies where cold business logic is sold as burning passion; free company clothing and low-cost company food; and company "values" made available in a dazzling display of collateral damage including wallet cards, T-shirts, posters, mouse pads, coffee cups and a company laptop bag to stuff it all into.

Okay, the *third* attempt is to trot out the carrots—money and the stuff money buys.

All of this is carefully calculated to work. It should work. Sometimes it seems like it works. It doesn't work. Not logically. Not neurobiologically.

HOW A MANAGER'S BRAIN WORKS. AND DOESN'T.

7

I N THE WORST corporate cultures, managers are expected to form stable, selfless, giving and forgiving relationships with companies that are ever-changing, selfish, greedy and unforgiving. These are companies where managers aren't afraid of losing their jobs; they're afraid of keeping them. Managers have often left even if they're still there.

This isn't working in a coal mine, but the impact is just as toxic— it's a soul mine. Hang a canary cage in any meeting room and the poor little thing would soon be wobbling unsteadily before collapsing claws-up in a pool of avian vomit. In these harshest of environments, managers make the conscious choice to fade back. They deliberately leave the best of who they are at home when they suit up every day for the detachment factory.

But in most corporate cultures, managers are there because they want to be there. They like their company. They want to help make things better. They want to take some sense of self from the might and magnificence of their organization. In many cases, managers don't even want to work less. They just want it to mean more.

Yet the same problem exists in these better environments and it's more dangerous because it's harder to see. Neurochemical markers in the brain identify options considered healthy and safe; these are the biological version of "values." If they can't be met, health and safety must be in jeopardy and the brain immediately shifts into threat containment mode. One of the protective processes it deploys is emotional detachment.

Try not to take this the wrong way, but your brain is smarter than you are.

◉   ◉   ◉

The human brain is comprised of three distinct regions, each a product of a separate moment in evolution. Think of this triune model as networked biological computers in constant communication, each with its own purpose, intelligence and programmed subjectivity The original, sitting atop the spinal cord, is the brain stem, or "lizard" brain, which controls the four F's: feeding, fighting, fleeing and fooling around.

As humans evolved, the brain did too, and it ultimately gave birth to the neocortex. The neocortex, or "rational" brain, is the part of the brain we think we think with. It's the newest part, and like anything new, we're most infatuated with it. Unfortunately, in this case, newest doesn't mean most useful. The neocortex organizes, categorizes, strategizes and performs a host of other analytical and conceptual functions.

But it doesn't make the big decisions.

Those decisions are mostly influenced by the limbic system, or "emotional" brain, which arrived on the scene between reptile and rational. The limbic system is the part of the brain that evalutates the reward potential of judgment calls, and it processes information

80,000 times faster than the neocortex. It's a prediction machine, wired to choose a decision with the highest probable return.

Key to the limbic operating system is something called the amygdala, bundles of neurons about the size and shape of an almond. There are two of them, idling in neutral but ever ready to be fast-sprung by one of two perceived possibilities: "This will help me" or "This will hurt me." The amygdala determines which neurochemicals the brain releases in response to either of these anticipated situations. It's not possible for the Help Me and Hurt Me responses to happen simultaneously; learning how to cause that is a different kind of book, bought at a different kind of bookstore.

Depending on the circumstances, these neurochemicals are released to push you either toward something or away from it. The brain marks and stores the information: *This Situation Meant That Action*. Memories exist to guide humans safely past the dangers of the unknown. Neurochemicals color memories and produce vivid subconscious drives about what to do in order to increase safety and cope with danger. Over time, neurochemical feedback loops are hardwired to help assure a rapid-fire response. When anything approaching that situation occurs again, the brain believes it knows which chemical cocktail to quickly mix and serve.

This process is what helps the brain make instinctively safe decisions in a constantly uncertain world. In turn, this helps to create values in a human being—the internal emotional compass.

The chemical energy released if the amygdala perceives "This will help me" includes: oxytocin, the neurohormone that mediates connection and trust; serotonin, which regulates well-being; and dopamine, the brain's sell-my-stereo-to-get-more-pleasure driver. These are coincidentally the principal chemicals released into the bloodstream by falling in love. They are self-regenerating motivational energy and the source of euphoric power. This is the chemistry that helps fuel and reinforce emotional commitment.

The brain is programmed for survival and recognizes that dopamine means health and safety. It creates the desire to do the things that will give it dopamine because dopamine is the sign that it's doing the best thing.

A bunch of chemicals are released if the amygdala perceives "This will hurt me" too, but in this case it's primarily adrenaline and cortisol, designed to help you rapidly back away from any environment or relationship considered harmful and avoid it at all costs in the future—get away, get mad or detach if avoidance isn't possible. This is fear-based energy, intended for short-term bursts, not extended use. It's toxic in sustained release; it eats itself and attempts to eat whomever it's energizing. Managers fueled by this type of energy are manic, multitasking, PDA-addicted change agents, but what's juicing them may be killing them at the same time. For sure, it's not allowing them to make healthy decisions for themselves, for others or for their company, and it's not allowing them to connect their jobs with life-affirming neurochemical reinforcement.

What would cause the amygdala to be stuck in "This will hurt me" in any manager's brain? An environment where they must subordinate personal values to better serve their company, forcing the brain to act against its best instincts for safety and well-being. Whenever the brain gets such a signal, the amygdala urgently assumes danger response mode and releases detachment chemicals. The limbic system's data warehouse duly catalogs this connection between action and chemical reaction to shorten response time should a similar circumstance ever again present itself If it's seen it before, it's going to try hard to avoid it again.

Given that a company demands to be the dominant organism in the relationship with its managers, it's likely that the amygdala in managers will regularly be sensing danger, releasing a steady stream of nasty, high-alert neurochemicals. If the company can cause the perception to change, it will access the positive self-reinforcement areas in managers' brains, automatically triggering all sorts of perky, high-commitment neurochemicals.

Review: Bad neurochemicals: Out. Good neurochemicals: In.

There is simply no way that external rewards can sustainably move the amygdala in managers. In fact, it's been repeatedly proven that external rewards can actually undermine internal motivation in human beings. Although external rewards are most used in a corporate environment, it's ironically what's most neurobiologically irrelevant to the motivation of the individual subjected to them. That's why companies always have to provide more carrots and bigger carrots and make jobs carrot-centric even for those managers who should reasonably be the most committed to overall company success.

The limbic system is about serious business and won't be lured by the promise of *shiny thing! shiny thing!* It can't be fooled by cheap substitutes, even if they're materially pretty valuable. To reliably trigger the desired limbic response in its manager population, a company would have to align the causes of oxytocin, serotonin and dopamine release with impeccable accuracy for each manager. The way to do that would be to connect life at work with health and safety: allow each manager to work according to their individual values.

Not reasonable for a company to have to do? Perhaps. But even the best corporate reasoning is meaningless to two-thirds of a manager's brain.

PINCH ME; I'M DREAMIN' 8

COMPANIES KNOW WHAT they want most: emotional commitment from managers. But they're nervous about the potential risk of gaining it and frustrated by sustained efforts that haven't produced sustained results. Your company is just trying to protect itself, but that prevents it from getting what it wants.

Managers know what they want most: to be allowed to achieve success by leveraging who they are, not by compromising it. But managers are detached and distracted by the constant effort of maintaining a personal center of gravity amidst a whirling corporate universe. You're just trying to protect yourself, but it prevents you from getting what you want.

Your dreams and the dreams of your company may be different, but they are in no way incompatible. The only problem seems to be that what your company wants most to receive it doesn't want to let you give, and what you want most to receive you don't want to give.

It's not just the emperor; nobody's wearing any clothes and, frankly, it's not all that attractive.

THE SOLUTION. CLEVERLY DISGUISED AS THE PROBLEM

What's needed is a model that will reliably allow managers to live their values at work without the company having to constantly facilitate the process. A self-sustaining model that is a safe and healthy choice for both the company and its managers. Brace yourself: The model is called leadership.

Wait—come back!

Not leadership the way you typically hear about it, as a corporate subversion of the concept—the 10, 100 or 1,000 immaculate and selfless organizational behaviors required for you to be anointed a "leader." The true purpose of leadership isn't to increase shareholder value or the productivity of work teams. That's important and leadership will indeed do these things when applied in an organization; any corporate objective that depends on inspired human effort will best be realized through leadership. But that's not the point of leadership; it never has been and it never will be, and to confuse cause and effect is to deny the critical reason to become a leader in the first place.

Taking the concept "leaders do the right thing" literally sets companies galloping off in an obsessive search for whatever "thing" is the Holy Grail of leadership. It's not what leaders do that's important; it's why they do it. Leadership is a motivation. It's a purpose before it's ever a practice. The worst thing in your own development as a leader is not to do it wrong. It's to do it for the wrong reasons.

There is more mythology, misdirection, superstition and generalized academic babble about leadership than any other business subject. In fact, the purpose of leadership is to change the world around you in the name of your values, so you can live those values more fully.

The process of leadership is to turn your values into a compelling cause for others, so you gain resources to help you do that. Real leadership is therefore the perfect organizing framework for gaining and delivering what we're talking about in *Bury My Heart at Conference Room B*.

The irreducible essence of leadership is that leaders are people who live their deepest personal values without compromise, and they use those values to make life better for others—this is why people become leaders and why people follow leaders.

Because leaders live their own values, they're essentially self-medicated—the pressure's off the company to provide the deepest motivational fulfillment. Leaders also remain the model of human beings driven to have emotional commitment and to create it in others, against all odds and, if necessary, against all protective common sense. It's real leaders that a company needs most if the organization is going to thrive.

Yet a company exists in a dangerous jungle; there are a lot of hungry heavy breathers lurking in the shadows. The constant focus is on survival, and the last thing it's going to chance is the counterintuitive move. What a company absolutely cannot do is knowingly introduce potential chaos into the organization, and this logically includes encouraging authentic leadership throughout its management ranks. At the root of chaos theory is the concept of the strange attractor, and leaders are most definitely your strange attractors.

Leadership in its truest form is seen as a hectic proposition, a messy thing and, for all its tempting benefits, uncertain and uncontrollable. How many times have you been told to be a leader, trained in one leadership method or another, preached at, screeched at, had leadership once again embedded in your job objectives? Yet how many times has it all stopped short of encouraging the uncompromising personal motivation that actually causes leadership in the first place? Companies want what leaders do without incurring why they do it.

Recognized or not, the intuitive corporate concern is that *real* leaders won't carry the company values wallet card; they'll carry their own and they'll burn the corporate house down in order to advance their cause. Allowing real leaders to thoroughly inhabit the system could destroy the system. They'll reorder the balance of power without considering practical consequences. This concern can be defined as: reasonable. That's what genuine, powerful leaders have often done throughout history.

But only if destroying the system was the purpose of their leadership. What if it were to protect the system? What if real leaders, transformed from throughout the ranks of a company's managers, flourished in the belief that to protect the company was to protect their ability to gain the personal benefits of leadership—to live their most important personal values every day at work?

Is this possible?

Any expert in human behavior will tell you that if you want an emotionally committed relationship then people must be allowed to be true to who they are in that relationship. This is the problem that companies must solve to get what they want most from their managers.

It's not a problem if the organizational structure just uses managers as standardized components with a ceiling of performance expectations. But if any company wants the best of what human beings can choose to give, it has to free them to give it. Only when a company sets its managers free will it have the dependable organization it dreams of. The company will finally be free as well. Free from the expensive burden of falsely stimulating shallow commitment. Managers will end up with what they've always wanted and so will the company.

New truth: The cause cannot always be the company; instead, it must also be managers' pursuit of their own values within the company. This isn't licensing chaos; it is ensuring control. There is no more reliable way for the company to become the cause than by not always insisting on being the cause.

Can companies trust their managers to remain committed to the enterprise if they're free to live their values at work? If you're managing managers, here's a sure way to tell: Could you trust yourself? If the answer is yes, the same trust can be extended throughout the management population of your company.

Human behavior is only unpredictable and dangerous if you don't start from humanity in the first place. To safely trust managers, a company must allow them to do the things that real leaders do for the reasons that real leaders do them. The company must allow itself to be the best possible place for managers to practice true fulfillment, to live their values and to realize deep connectivity and purpose.

This is the system managers will protect. This is the system managers dream about.

GOOD NEWS: IT'S NOT YOUR FAULT
BAD NEWS: IT'S YOUR RESPONSIBILITY

Your company won't naturally align itself with your deepest personal values; you have to align with your own values and then make them work within the company. You have to become that real leader.

Can you do it? Oh, *yeah*. Leadership isn't some rare genetic imperative. It's innate in every human being and it's damn well innate in you; you just have to know where to get started. Leaders begin with an acute awareness of what's most important to them and a deep desire to remake the world around them so they can more fully experience it. This awareness in history's greatest leaders has typically started with their personal values being put under extreme pressure. You want to know if something is important to you? Meet someone trying to take it away.

Nelson Mandela? Mother Teresa? History's greatest leaders had it easy. Pop quiz: Freedom: Yes or No? Leprosy: Good or Bad?

The conditions necessary to ignite your own leadership are already in place because what's important to you is under pressure too. But it may be harder to realize because the pressure on a manager's personal values often arrives gift-wrapped, with financial reinforcement and a sense of self, gained by affiliating with the purpose and power of your company.

Remember, too, that your company doesn't really want you to be a leader. Leaders use their own values and vision to overthrow the established order and set people free. What are ya, *nuts*? That's the last thing your company wants you to be capable of or interested in. Your company just wants you to do the things that leaders do, like model selfless acts of devotion and inspire a group of sullen individuals to make a bloody charge up the competitor's hill to capture the fourth-quarter flag.

What your company really wants is for you to make an emotional commitment to your job, not just a financial, intellectual and physical commitment. Nothing wrong with that, but that's not why you should be a leader. Listen up: As a manager, your most important responsibility is to your company. As a leader, your most important responsibility is to yourself. You must fulfill your personal responsibility first; far from being subversive, this is the single most supportive corporate action you can take.

Your company really has to work for you before you'll really work for your company.

BUSTING THE BIG MYTH

Who are the happiest people? Those who are doing work they believe in. Those who live in a safe place because they can count on the support of others for what matters most to them. This potential is there for you and always has been, buried underneath all the mangling and misinformation about leadership.

One of the biggest myths of leadership is that it's a burden. If it were a burden, nobody would do it. It's a benefit. Beyond that, it's a series of profound personal benefits that you can get only by doing what leaders do. You're going to love the benefits of leadership.

It's time now for you to get started. You're going to make the job much better for yourself and you're going to take your company right along with you. It's time to finally learn not just exactly how to *be* a leader but exactly *why*: It's time to understand the real power of leadership to change the world. To change a manager's world.

You can live your deepest personal values at work. Yes, your company will let you and, yes, your employees will help you. I'm about to show you the method that will allow you to do it and to ensure that it's supported on both ends.

It all starts with values. Let's get you some.

And the river opens for the righteous . . .

—STEVEN VAN ZANDT

PART 3
YOU MUST.
YOU CAN.

That was the river.

This is the sea.

—MIKE SCOTT

HOW TO DECIDE WHAT'S TRULY MOST IMPORTANT TO YOU

9

WHAT ARE YOUR VALUES?

George Carlin had a great line about driving: It doesn't matter what speed you're going; anybody moving slower than you is an idiot, anybody moving faster than you is a maniac. So it seems lately with the concept of values, which have become an ideological demarcation point—loose vs. tight, dark vs. light, wrong vs. right.

The transformation of values into fence building and social weaponry happens when they're confused with morals. Morals—how a person ought to act in the opinion of authority, consensus or the popularly interpreted rules of society—are the right thing to do. Values are the right thing for you to do.

Your values may sometimes be the same as your morals, but they don't have to be for you to have both. You may think it's morally wrong to steal, but it isn't something you care about obsessively and that drives your daily decision making *(Note to self: put it back)*. It isn't a value.

Values are deeply held personal beliefs that form your own priority code for living. Doesn't exactly lend itself to an acronym, but there you have it. They're the individual biases that allow you to decide which actions are true for you alone. They're the personal standards that give you the most and that you care about the most. They're the definition of what life looks like when you live it exactly the way you want to. Values are your very own source of safety, hope and renewal.

WHERE ARE YOUR VALUES?

Being a leader means being able to sell your values to others. The easiest thing right now would be to give you a superfast way to do that—a superfast track to trouble. If you're not sure what you want to sell, learning a powerful way to sell it isn't a real good idea. Some patience—granted, a great quality in *other* people—is required to ensure that your choice of values is the right choice. If it's the right choice, the people who buy your values will help you live life the way you really want to live it.

Where do your values come from?

- Early upbringing
- Big decisions and the consequences of those decisions
- Personal beliefs and priorities placed under extreme pressure
- Religious and spiritual doctrines
- Intimate mentors and role models
- Significant life events
- www.tellmemyvalues.com

The most profound method for understanding your—wait a minute: the tellmemyvalues.com thing was a *joke*; get back here—deepest values is called Life. Other good methods:

- You can look at a list of common human values and see which resonate the strongest. I've included a list for you here and it's the best place to start.
- You can consider the influences that can easily obscure or subvert your true values. I've included a description of the major influences for you.
- You can ask yourself questions both tough and tender. I've included a process for you.
- You can look at your life. The decisions you've made, the ones you've consciously or instinctively avoided and the road nobody but you has seriously considered traveling. I've included a method for you.
- You can talk to others. Ask the mentors and the inspirations in your life about how they first realized what was truly important to them. I've included different ways for you to enter those discussions.
- You can listen to others. Do people close to you keep saying they know you better than you know yourself? Make them prove it. I've included a list of questions to give others a foundation for response.
- You can do all of these things. You knew that was coming.

STEP ONE: PICK FROM THIS LIST

▶ HOW TO DO IT

1. Examine the Fifty Values on the Following Pages

You might recognize or covet many of them.

2. Choose the Ten Values That Mean the Most to You

Grab some paper and a pen. Identify the ten values that mean the most to you personally, not just the ones you think make you look good. Choose them if they're important to you, even if you're not always living them. It's a pretty big list of pretty big values, but if it doesn't include personal priorities, come up with your own.

You'll notice that "market share" is not on this list. These are your personal values, the ones that you had long before you came to the job of management and that you'll have long after.

Over the years, I've watched managers engage in complex rationalizations as they're asked to make this choice. "Ooh, 'Power' is on the list! I want power. "I see 'Spirituality' is on the list, too. I guess I have to pick that instead. Wait a minute—spirituality sort of means believing in a higher power! I'll take 'Power.'"

Choose the ones that work for you and don't worry about it. There are no wrong values on the list.

3. Define the Meaning of Each of the Ten Values You've Chosen

I've included one possible definition for each of these values—in case you're unfamiliar with the word "cooperation," for example. If the given definition doesn't work for you, change it until it does.

4. Take No More Than Ten Minutes to Do It—Set Your Watch

There's a reason for this, as you'll see. You'll have plenty of time later to review your choices.

My Value	One Definition
1. Accomplishment	Succeeding in reaching goals
2. Advancement	Progress, promotion, improvement
3. Adventure	Taking risks, new experiences
4. Affection	Love, deep friendship
5. Altruism	Helping those who cannot help themselves
6. Balance	Calm, moderate, perspective
7. Commitment	Dedication to cause, satisfaction in obligation
8. Compassion	Empathy, tolerance and understanding of others

My Value	One Definition
9. Competence	Do things well, consistent self-improvement
10. Competitiveness	Besting performance in yourself or others
11. Control	Influence or direct people's behavior, course of events
12. Cooperation	Pulling together for a common goal, support of others
13. Courage	Testing limits, facing difficulties with resilience
14. Creativity	Imagination, new ways of doing and seeing
15. Curiosity	Sense of wonder, awe about the world
16. Determination	Strength and perseverance, whatever it takes
17. Enlightenment	Pursuit of awareness that feeds the soul
18. Equality	Protection of equivalent status, rights opportunities
19. Fairness	Equal consideration, value of the greater good
20. Family	Mutual support and growth
21. Freedom	Independence, free will
22. Fun	Enjoyment, playfulness, sense of play
23. Harmony	Oneness, alignment
24. Health	Well-being of mind, body and spirit
25. Humor	Cleverness, stress-relieving perspective
26. Impact	Making a difference, changing the world, creating legacy
27. Individuality	Originality, self-expression
28. Innovation	Creating something new, better, different
29. Influence	Persuasion, bringing others together around common cause
30. Integrity	Honor, honesty, strength of character
31. Intelligence	Acquiring and applying knowledge

My Value	One Definition
32. Involvement	Being "present" and participating fully
33. Joy	Appreciating the extraordinary in everyday things
34. Learning	Continuing education and experiences
35. Loyalty	Remaining faithful to a person or cause
36. Order	Respect for procedure and organization, calm
37. Passion	Enthusiasm, powerful attraction
38. Peace	Calm, centered, free from stress
39. Power	Ability to influence people and conditions
40. Recognition	Attention, positive notice
41. Relationships	Connection with others
42. Respect	Fair treatment, valuing individuals for uniqueness and opinion
43. Responsibility	Sense of duty, responsibility, conscientiousness
44. Security	Financial and/or emotional stability
45. Service	To be of assistance and support to a person or cause
46. Spirituality	Moral compass, belief in higher purpose, faith
47. Stability	Predictability and steadiness
48. Teaching	Passing knowledge on to others
49. Tradition	Support for known customs and beliefs
50. Wisdom	Application of knowledge and experience

Was it easy to choose your top ten values from a long list? Good for you. Was it hard to choose your top ten values from a long list? Good for you. Either way is perfectly understandable and completely irrelevant.

You're going to need to take a stand on just a few values. The longer your own list of values, the less able you're going to be to even remember it, let alone get anyone else to. Stick with the few that are the most important to you; your life will be mighty fine if you can meet even some of your top values at work.

1. Cut Your List of Ten Values to Five

Pick the five values that most define you as a human being.

2. Take No More Than Five Minutes to Do It

You'll have plenty of time later to review your choices.

Was it easy to choose your top five values from a long list? Good for you. Was it hard to choose your top five values from a long list? Good for you.
Uh-oh.
That's right, you need to make one more cut. This time from the five that you just couldn't live without to the three that absolutely, more than anything, define you as an individual human being. And you need to do it in three minutes.
Yes, it's an artificial construct; no doubt you personally embody an infinite list of admirable values. However, my ultimate purpose is to get you the same results that history's greatest leaders have gotten by translating what they've done intuitively into a series of practical tactics. Leaders maintain an intense focus on a few things—you know what they care about and they show a marked lack of interest in anything they don't care about. Think eating habits of a cat.
Relax, this is the last cut you have to make; otherwise, you'd end up with no values, which is where you might have started. We don't have time for that kind of Zen poetry—we've got your leadership platform to build.

1. Cut Your List of Five to Three

Pick the three values you just couldn't live without.

2. Take No More Than Three Minutes to Do It

You'll have plenty of time later to review your choices.

STEP TWO:
CONSIDER THE CONSIDERABLE INFLUENCES

Quick: What are your top values?

It wouldn't take any real leader long to answer this question, yet in *Bury My Heart at Conference Room B* interviews, many managers presented with the seemingly simple question you just answered find to their amazement that they can't immediately say. Many of the managers who can immediately say change their minds several times upon further reflection. Many wonder whether they should have just picked "Flexibility" as a value and quit while they were ahead.

Are you sure that the values you chose in less than twenty minutes are really your top three? Would you be amazed if they weren't?

Not being able to easily confirm your own top values is nothing to be amazed about—it would be more amazing if you could. It's tough for anyone to live a life of consciously chosen values in today's world. Understanding why is a significant move toward understanding the values themselves and protecting yourself from outside attempts at manipulating what's most important to you.

There's an intimate connection between your emotions and your strong opinions about the way things ought to be. It's impossible to separate your emotions from your values because one keeps influencing the other. The big question is, *what influences both of them?*

The answer is a whole lot of things and all at the same time. You are being played, constantly, often by groups who are better resourced and harder working than you are. There is constant persuasive pressure—some tempting, some threatening, some overt, some covert—intended to steer you away from self-awareness. When you're not on your own agenda, you're prey to the agenda of others. Anybody who has a role for you—be it as customer, constituent, citizen, partner, parent or most certainly as manager—stands to profit if you don't know your own values.

This isn't always intentionally wicked; some of it is from commercial interests but some of it is just human nature. Regardless, the result is the same: When you don't know what's true for you, everyone else has unusual influence.

▶ LIFE BEGINS

The first place you get values is from your family, when you're only a wee beastie and too young to do anything more than gobble what's been given in the faith that it's good for you. You may indeed be the lucky beneficiary of solid, positive values that you would have chosen even if they hadn't been imprinted on you. Or not: All families flirt with dysfunctionality, but some like to go all the way.

Either way, this happens before you realize it, so you may not be aware that most of your ensuing adult behavior, regardless of how healthy, focused and supportive of others it is—or how self-punishing, erratic and entertaining to others it is—is purposeful.

Most people don't really question the script they're acting from. Even if you do and find you have every reason to rewrite your character's motivation, it's not an easy challenge to take on. Your values have already begun to define your reality and form self-justification for your actions. Plus, there could be a deep-seated fear that you'll lose attachment to your parents if you conflict with their values. It's not like you could have left home and easily changed your values like changing your laundry. They'd keep finding their way back home, just like your laundry.

▶ LIFE ON SALE

Consumerism is essentially based on making someone feel small in order to sell them something that makes them feel big.

Did you really need to buy the brand of clothing and jewelry you wear, the car you drive or the house you live in? Could you have gotten away with a cheaper, generic, more practical version of most of it? Something—maybe the 2,500 commercial messages that the average adult is exposed to each week—got to you and made you believe you needed these things to confirm that you are more popular, likeable, attractive, powerful, successful, accepted, smarter or hipper. This isn't just you—thankfully you can't see that I'm writing this from a desk surrounded by fabulous stuff I don't need, suspicious that it has already been replaced by something new that I don't need even more . . . and so must have immediately.

This kind of stimulation doesn't last because it's not built to. It's built to give you a short-term high that you'll return for again and again. Not that there's anything wrong with *stuff*; it often feels good and, even though money clearly isn't synonymous with taste, it often looks good. But when rewards come from an external source instead of an internal source, they're unreliable, which means they're dangerous if you grow to depend on them.

▶ LIFE DURING OUR TIME

Like you need a book to tell you: Things are tense outside. Time was when you could wake up in the morning to the local news, view the bizarre atrocities committed by neighbor against neighbor while you slept, and think, "We've got to get out of this city. We've got to move to the country." Now, after sending the day's last e-mail at midnight, you can hit the news online and instantly see that war is ongoing in twenty-seven countries. It seems wherever you go you can't get away.

Strange things happen to you if you're frightened without first having a strong grip on what you believe in. Your values can seem like an indulgent luxury in times of widespread problems—especially if you've been convinced it's necessary to surrender your opinions to protect the larger ideal. Or it can seem a reasonable decision to allow the larger ideal to let you off the hook for deciding your own values.

A frightened culture assigns the leadership mantle to anyone who promises them safety; sometimes those people are true leaders who deliver on that promise, but sometimes our willingness to delegate a safe way home is the surest way to lose what will protect us the most— our own sense of self.

▶ LIFE ON THE JOB

Being a manager today is more than ever—more to get but more you have to do to get it. The morphing of a manager's job from physical to intellectual means the boundaries are harder to guard; work follows you home and easily vaults the fence into the rest of your life. Take a vacation? Many managers would rather stay at work and let work take a vacation.

Corporate rewards are based on getting things for doing things; there is no bounty for feeling things. Sometimes that's what management is—a feeling. A feeling that your job doesn't exactly have a sleep-over relationship with reality.

You're expected to hire, train and motivate the very best talent when they're not around to be hired, you don't have time to train them and you don't have the tools to motivate them. You're expected to constantly explain strategies to others when those strategies haven't been fully explained to you and then represent those strategies with your own good name when they come and go without coherent explanation. You're expected to constantly sell your people on the value of change when that change clearly has no value for them whatsoever.

Oh, great, and then *after* lunch you can single-handedly repave the entire company parking lot.

Your career wasn't built to handle the full weight of your emotional satisfaction. Work is purpose, and accomplishment of goals is confirmation of your special abilities and extra effort. It's good to have management responsibility, to do your job well and be recognized for it. But fulfilling your responsibilities isn't the same as fulfilling your values.

▶ THAT'S LIFE

You're not dumb just because you may be a little numb. We live in numbing, unconscious societies and often don't sense the danger anymore. Constant paper cuts to the soul go unnoticed and untreated, infecting our true sense of self. The contemporary way of thinking prizes not being tested—we respect things that are easy. Most people live in dread at the thought of yet another "learning experience."

Why are we so afraid to know ourselves? Because we think we won't be enough. Admittedly, that's not an unreasonable fear: Everybody might not like or understand the real you, and people shoot people they don't like and don't understand.

Do you ever really change your values? Sometimes, but not as often as you might imagine—mostly you just allow them to catch up with you. Even if you once prowled the wild streets all night as Ziggy Stardust and now prowl the spreadsheets all night as your company's vice president of acquisitions, you're still the same person underneath. What might have changed isn't that you've found your values at last but that you have at last let your values find you. This is perhaps the single upside to maturity, a fundamentally ironic concept that finally allows you to do all of the things you're now too busy, exhausted or intelligent to do.

It's possible that your values haven't been called into play yet. You may have had a healthy family upbringing but it took the birth of your own child to bring this value to the fore, inspiring you to continue your family's example of a loving and supporting environment. If you'd define your early days as more of a downgrading than an upbringing, the birth of a child may cause that family value to assert itself as a passionate commitment to filling in what was sadly missing from your own young life.

Unfortunately, there's no law against being smart and living stupid, no matter how harmful it may be to you. You can unknowingly ricochet away from your deepest values because you've mistakenly come to believe you don't deserve to live them—and spend much of your life sabotaging what you want most by aiming for just the opposite. This doesn't mean your values haven't always been your values. They're driving you still and they're waiting for you still. Toss them away as forcefully as you want, then duck: *boomerang*.

STEP THREE: CONFIRM YOUR CHOICE

You could conceivably change your choice of top values at any time, although I wouldn't suggest making it part of a regular Monday to-do list, which would only confuse your people. *"You, there—what are you doing? Oh, you're still on the 'Harmony' value. You must have been out last week when I changed it to 'Ruthless Domination.'"* Much better to know that those values are not easily open to revision but are instead a true representation of your deepest beliefs.

Ask yourself these seemingly innocent questions to further check on your choice of values. We're done with the Gandhi Invitational Speed Trials; take as much time as you want from here on.

COFFEE WITH MICHAEL SPENCE

The winner of the Nobel Prize in Economics and former dean of the Stanford Graduate School of Business leans over the table to impart apparently urgent information. "I've got to tell you, Stan, winning the Nobel Prize will change your life."

Gee, thanks for the heads-up, Mike. Just in time, too.

"And I'll tell you something else," he says.

I bend closer, hoping to snuff up some secondhand Nobel wisdom.

"The most important things in life are the things we get the least help in learning how to do," he states emphatically. "Sooner or later, a manager crosses the line when they're going to be considered for their legacy and their impact as a mentor, a teacher able to pass their own values on to someone else. There are a lot of people in management positions absolutely ill-equipped to do this.

"We definitely own some of the problem in B-schools," he admits. "We don't prepare people at anywhere near the level of emotional sophistication you advocate. The academic side attacks any curriculum that causes people to think about their own interpersonal interactions, their own testimony and the relationships they have with others, or to increase the depth of the way they think about these things. Besides," he adds, "people don't respond very well when we put organizational behaviors into the curriculum. They could care less. They want to learn finance, marketing, money, power and status.

"These people graduate and take enormously important management positions. If they didn't come into their careers with a strong sense of self, the ability to validate their own values and get that satisfaction, where are they going to pick it up? They're going to seek a life force wherever they can get it, and in a company some of those places are dangerous because they're not real and not healthy. You get turned around by not knowing yourself."

He gazes into the distance. "It doesn't matter how smart you are when that happens. It's hard to find your way home."

• • •

► HOW TO DO IT

1. Answer for Each of Your Top Three Values

Be sure to answer all fifteen questions.

2. Confirm the Strength of Your Preference

Rate your answer to each question on a scale of 1 to 10, 10 being the strongest—*Oh, yeah*—and 1 being the least—*Nah.*

3. Total the Numerical Score

4. Check the Meaning of Your Score

At the end of the questions see if you've confirmed each value as being key to your personal fulfillment.

1	2	3	4	5	6	7	8	9	10
Disagree									Agree

1. My most treasured accomplishments have to do with living this value.
2. The time I remember feeling most trapped has to do with not living this value.
3. I am most thrilled when people compliment me for displaying this value.
4. If people strongly advised me not to advocate this value, I'd do it anyway.
5. Those people I admire most have (or seem to have) this value.
6. If I knew for sure that I wouldn't be able to meet this value in my life, I'd go seriously nuts.
7. I admit it: I believe people who don't understand the importance of this value are at best clueless and more likely of diminished capacity.

8. There was a time I really failed to protect this value and it still haunts me.
9. My friends would bet I'd rage on and on about this value given even the slightest provocation.
10. I've had big trouble in relationships because this value was in conflict.
11. The best decisions I've made for myself supported this value.
12. The most memorable disagreement I've ever had was ultimately about this value.
13. If I were going to make a list of the ideal characteristics of a partner—and by answering this question I'm not saying I've ever done that—this value would be one of the first things I'd put on the list. I mean, I don't have a list, but . . .
14. The worst decisions I've made for myself violated this value.
15. On the days that I feel life is too short, I resolve to live this value more fully.

► YOUR TOTAL SCORE FOR EACH VALUE

135–150: Core

You feel strongly about this value and it's probably a part of your personal code for living. Still, it's a good idea to take the confirmation step that follows. One can never be too smugly convinced that they're evolved.

120–134: Strong

This value is a strong preference for you, but another may be even stronger. There are no "right" values; "right" is what works for you, and choosing your top three doesn't mean others aren't extremely important to you. Don't let such a concern cause you to prioritize against instinct—go with those few you couldn't imagine living without. Check especially the cuts from top ten to five and from top five to top three.

. . .

105–119: Unsure

There are values more important to you than this one. Back to the list of fifty with you and let's try it again. Spend some more time on that list and push back on your initial assumptions. Don't feel bad about this: You're not smarter just because you can instantly pick your most important values; this process is enough to give anyone pause and/or hives.

15–104: Special

Did you use darts to pick your values?

STEP FOUR: CONNECT THE MOMENTS OF TRUTH

Sometimes awareness of a value is crystallized in one event. Oftentimes, it's honed by years of experience. Sometimes its genesis is positive. Oftentimes, although we gloat about nibbling from the higher branches, it's the negative that finally captures our dim-witted attention.

One of the best ways to confirm your values is to understand where those values came from—understand the moment, or moments, of truth that caused them to become personal priorities. This awareness is consistent in every successful leader: They don't just know what their values are, they know why.

Here's one example of how Moments of Truth can create values that last forever. I know these particular moments to be true because this is the story of how my own values were formed. I offer it to help you realize how you might have first formed your own.

HOW I LEARNED MY OWN VALUES

These days, I live in San Francisco, the kind of town where people love to claim their earliest memory is of being in the womb. (What—it was *dark*? Go away.) My own earliest memory was of being seven years old; I remember it like it was yesterday.

In those days, we lived in a big apartment complex in Los Angeles. I was an only child and used to walk to school with the big kid from across the hall. One morning, I had a hand on the front door ready to leave when my mother bent down to clasp the other. She said, "I'm not going to be here when you get home from school today. I'm going into the hospital for some tests, but I'll be back in a few days." I'm not sure I knew exactly what she meant, but I got that she was going away. Still, she assured me everything would be fine, so I left for school. I didn't see her again for four years.

During that time she suffered through thirteen major surgeries. Through no fault of her own, she used up our entire major medical insurance and bankrupted our family.

This left my father with few options. He hated his job—was an engineer before it was hip or profitable—but couldn't quit. Preexisting conditions made any new employer's insurance coverage impossible, and my mother's doctors were emphatic that she'd be dead within a month if transferred from a private to a county hospital. He not only had to stay on the job but work as much overtime as possible, desperately trying to cover all the bills our remaining insurance didn't. More time was spent meeting with doctors and sitting by his unconscious wife's bedside in intensive care. There was no time left to take care of a seven-year-old boy and no brothers or sisters to help. I was sent to live in a foster home.

If you have young children, you know they're egocentric: They have limited perspective, believe the world revolves around them and personalize everything. Despite every reassurance, a young child in a troubled family will be sure they're at fault for all the trouble. I was sure that my mother being so sick, my family being torn apart and my being in such a horrible place was somehow my fault. I just didn't know which of the many sins I committed on a regular basis at seven years old was responsible. I couldn't understand how to fix the problem on my own and couldn't get any help: I was too young to visit my mom in the hospital, I saw my dad every few weeks and he was doing his best to *not* tell me what was going on, I had no siblings to explain things to me, and foster homes aren't in the information business.

Two of the very bad things that can happen to a little kid: They can discover the people who love them the most can't protect them or they can discover that they can't protect the people whom they love the most. I got both, couldn't prevent it, couldn't fix it, and so I shut down. I withdrew completely, stopped talking and stopped listening. And stopped being a kid in a foster home. I started becoming a problem kid in a foster home.

Foster homes don't like problems, so I was kicked out, which didn't do my sense of well-being much good. I shut down even further and was sent to another, then another and another. By the time I got to the seventh foster home, I hadn't made a sound or eye contact for over a month and had to be lifted from the car in a fetal ball. This one foster home cared enough to accept me provisionally while they determined if they could safely house me long-term, since it seemed possible that I had some sort of rapidly deteriorating condition, which nobody could explain. They quickly ordered every diagnostic test that somebody would pay for. When the results of one of those tests arrived, it changed my life and taught me my first core value.

It was an IQ test that bizarrely enough scored at some sort of genius level. This meant nothing to me, but it sure meant something to the foster home. Amidst the many children afflicted with learning disabilities deposited in such places, here was one of their own who had "made good."

I didn't know anything about that stuff; all I knew was that from the day the test came back I began to get extra recognition and reinforcement. I was routinely dragged into meetings and urged to "say something intelligent" for the amazement of staff or important visitors. I was just your typical ignorant kid but found if I said something that evidently sounded intelligent, I could get plenty of special treatment, sometimes including a Snickers bar. Baby, I went to work.

Desperate to remain in the spotlight, I hunted for reliable sources of adult wisdom to call my own. This is where I mostly learned to read, and before I left that foster home years later I had read every book they had— books I didn't understand and books I clearly had no business reading. My book of choice was the encyclopedic *Physician's Desk Reference* because it contained the longest sentences with the longest words. I'd copy the description of horrific side effects from some rare treatment for liver disorders, draw little code animals on the back, tear the paper into a few pieces and approach different staff asking them to sound out each piece for me. At night I'd put the pieces together and rehearse. The next morning I'd waddle—adorably—into a staff meeting, projectile-vomit the absurd information, grab my candy bar and go.

These experiences gave me Intelligence as a core value and taught me that intelligence can definitely improve quality of life. Yet to me intelligence has never been a matter of being born with a high or low IQ. It's an acquisition process: I believe how someone gets smart and stays smart decides their intelligence.

Intelligence helped me back then, but it didn't change my reality: I was still stuck in that foster home. That's when I learned my second core value.

A small child is granted no power in their world, no ability to rationally influence events. It's the kind of thing that will drive a human of any size nuts, and children seek to shape and predict their world any way they can. One of the ways is to make complex deals with God or any other supernatural beings believed to be vested with omnipotence and a willingness to deal. Ongoing negotiations with Valhalla—"If I do this for you, you'll do this for me"—sound like, "If I'm a good boy and I eat all my vegetables, my mom will get well and my parents will come and take me away from this horrible place."

I started to live in a world of my own devising and learned that Creativity was a value. More to the point, I learned that creativity can save your life. It can give you answers to problems you can't solve with just the facts at hand, no matter how you array them.

Finally came the day my mother got well enough to return home and at that point my family established its own clear priorities: 1) keep her alive and out of the hospital, 2) allow my parents to reconnect after not being able to spend time together for years, and 3) me. Sounds great— only three priorities and you made the short list—until you realize that it's "One, two, you." My family had urgent issues and, although they loved me, the minute drama of my daily life wasn't always one of them. Which is when I discovered my third core value: I had to Accomplish more than the average kid if I wanted to be seen.

My first strategy was to accomplish as much trouble as is humanly possible. It was successful—sort of—and my mother made up for the lost years by being at school more than I was. Soon noting the severe blowback factor, I switched directions, applied the same accomplishment ethic and went from detention to the honor society in a semester. I never graduated high school, but this Accomplishment value has been with me ever since. It's allowed me to be very successful, but it's not always very pretty: Everything has to constantly be bigger, better, faster, more challenging.

A lot of values are important to me now as an adult. Taking care of my Family—and anyone whom I consider family—is a sacred opportunity, and I intentionally overreact to any perceived threat. I'm obsessive about Health, have fourteen insurance policies, take eighteen vitamin supplements three times a day and have turned our entire garage into a commercial-quality gym. My mother was chained to a hospital bed, my father to a job he hated, and so Freedom is a driving force; I get hot real quick about any oppression, personal or world condition. I've seen the results of not having financial Security and never take it lightly. I consider Integrity— especially accountability—fundamental to any relationship and regularly drive everybody, especially myself, nuts about it.

Yet when push comes to shove, the values that mean the most remain Intelligence, Creativity and Accomplishment. I'm not saying they're right or wrong, they just . . . are. I'm not saying that they should be your top values. This is only my story and yours is the one that's important here.

■ ■ ■

Elaine Hope Slap fought for life with all she had. She ultimately survived thirty-two major operations, passing away two months after her eightieth birthday, while this book was being written. As someone who faced death and survived it many times, she learned things about living that the rest of us don't know. This is what she'd want to tell you: Don't ever give up on anything or anyone you believe in; always stop to watch the sun shine, the bird hop, the child play; and judge your accomplishments by your own standards, not the world's.

► HOW TO DO IT

1. Go Back as Far as Possible in Your Life

Search for the Moment of Truth. Identify the pivotal points that forged each of your top three values for you.

2. Look for the Choices You've Made

What are the decisions that first caused you to need your values or first become aware of them?

3. Don't Panic

If you can't easily connect a Moment of Truth in your life to your choice of top values, it may mean that you haven't been conscious of the value and can't immediately make a connection between actions and intentions. Just search a bit longer; it's a healthy process. If you really didn't have a single Moment of Truth in your entire life, *that* would be a Moment of Truth. As well as some sort of tax credit.

STEP FIVE: TALK TO YOURSELF, THEN TALK TO OTHERS

"The unexamined life is not worth living," said Socrates. Spoken like a guy who didn't have quarterly numbers to hit in the middle of a reduction in force. Becoming your own philosophical proctologist may be one agenda item too many in your real-world management schedule.

Wait a minute: Turns out Socrates was right. And if you want one of those lives worth living, identifying your most important values is a good place to start.

Know thyself isn't a new concept; it was first inscribed on the Temple of Apollo at Delphi in the sixth century BC, and a version of the same sentiment has appeared for years on urban alley walls. One of the best ways to know yourself is by being relentlessly Socratic—see how these paragraphs tie elegantly together? On the next pages are questions to help you in your own Socratic process if you're unsure—or intrigued—about your values and why they mean so much.

► HOW TO DO IT

1. Explore What You Believe In

Use any or all of the questions here to identify patterns of choices made, directions taken and options refused in favor of others. See how they map to your choice of values; if they don't seem to, go back to the original list and explore your choices.

2. Ask These Same Questions of Those Who Know You Best

Choose those who will give you the most objective feedback. Remember that the perceptions others have of you depend on how you behave, but how you behave may not always be a reflection of your true values. Talk to them only after you've listened to yourself.

Beginnings

■ What were the values of my family that made me feel safe and loved?

- When was the first time I decided on values different from my parents?
- When was the first time I decided that I needed values?

Challenges

- Have my values ever been challenged or threatened? How did I react?
- When am I at my most unreasonable—most unwilling to consider another point of view?
- What choices have I made to protect my values?

Decisions

- What is the hardest decision I've ever made that felt the best?
- What are the three biggest decisions I've ever made?
- If I had all the money I wanted, how would I be spending my time?

Good Times

- What is the most beautiful thing in my life?
- When have I been most at peace?
- What seems to come naturally to me?

Bad Times

- What has been most unfair in my life?
- Other than death or serious injury, what's the worst that could happen to me and why would this be so bad?
- What are some things that have memorably driven me crazy that I still can't stop obsessing about?

Messages to the World

- What would the world look like if I could create it?
- What's wrong with the world that must change?

- If I could say anything to the president of my country, what would it be?

Endings

- What is the legacy I want to be known for?
- What are the three things most important to living a fulfilled life that I would tell a child?
- If I could do it all over, what do I wish I'd known sooner and why?

SWEAT TIME AT MICROSOFT
true tales from the *bury my heart* files

Check the *Oxford Dictionary of the English Language* under "aggressive" and you'll find Orlando Ayala's picture. The head of worldwide sales for Microsoft is a slim, good-looking Colombian who sports a casual Caesar haircut—the haircut being the only casual thing about him. He vibrates with coiled intensity; you sense he's friendly unless he senses you're edible. Now the guy famous for donning combat gear to whip his sales teams into a feral frenzy has pulled his top managers together for two days of *Bury My Heart at Conference Room B* and asked that I facilitate it personally.

The event is to be held at a local hotel when, at the last minute, Orlando switches it to a meeting room on the Microsoft campus in Redmond. I don't realize the dangerous significance of this, but his managers sure do.

Orlando's direct reports are all big gunslingers themselves, running organizations with billions of dollars in revenue responsibility and thousands of people. You'd expect them to be confident enough to handle the provocative message of *Bury My Heart at Conference Room B,* yet as we head into the first morning it becomes clear something is wrong. Plenty of averted eyes, anxious shuffling and nervous laughter—it's starting to make *me* nervous. I stop to ask, "What, exactly, is the problem?"

"It's this room," they mutter. "You don't know this room. We know this room. We call it The Slaughterhouse. This is where Orlando brings us to beat on us about our sales performance. We can hear the screams; we can see the blood dripping down the walls."

Oh, fabulous. And here I am telling them to get in touch with their groovy selves and bring the best of who they are to work. It's like telling a bunch of cows to get in touch with their groovy selves and bring the best of who they are to McDonald's.

We wobble on but things are still way off. I say, tell me your core values as human beings. They respond with the likes of "Freedom," "Spirituality," "Altruism." I say, now pretend I'm one of your employees and tell me what that means to me. They respond with the likes of "I have core values of Freedom, Spirituality and Altruism. So where are we going, my people? We are going to whack the *snot* out of sales projections! We are going to crush anyone in our way like the *insects* they are! What you need to do is work *harder*, work *faster* and work *more!*"

Sigh. Let's try it again. Take 17.

The next morning I tell them to go ahead and call security now because I'm not leaving until they get it. If you really want to meet sales and revenue targets, you have to bring your personal values to work, I insist—for yourselves and for the company. We move further, dig deeper and at last the room shifts; everyone can feel the message finally sink in. "I'll never be able to see my job the same way again," says one, shaking her head, and others, markedly including Orlando, agree.

Game. Set. Match. *Whew*.

The next day

Microsoft is a juicy new client for my company, and since I had to be in Redmond anyway I've agreed to stay and facilitate another session later that week for a different group. On the day in between I'm talking with Mike Creamer, Orlando's business manager, when Orlando walks up. "The last two days have had a lot of impact on me," he says. "I want you to put some thoughts together about how it can impact the entire company."

"That was nice," I offer after he leaves. "I should do that."

"He means do it now," Mike advises. "Orlando's leaving early tomorrow morning for a strategic planning session with Bill Gates and Steve Ballmer and wants to take it with him."

I don't get to the hotel until about 11:00 that night, when I remember I've promised Orlando the e-mail. I start fooling around with some rough-draft thoughts and . . . get *into* it. What begins as basic recommendations soon becomes a blazing indictment about every wrong move made that I think poses a threat to Microsoft's continued viability as the leading market contender. At one point, I write, "There isn't an empire in history that thought they were going to fall before they fell."

"That's *good*," I say out loud and, brimming with positive self-reinforcement, continue to feverishly type away. Not that I have any intention of sending any of it; I'm just warming up the laptop.

"You know what your problem is, Orlando . . . ?" I pound out, nodding and cackling to myself.

Hours later, I've finally got it all out of my system. I lean back to stretch before starting on the real e-mail. And watch in horror as some deviant muscle memory causes a finger to leap up entirely of its own accord and press the Send button.

OhmyGOD!

Great. Just great. What seemed like pithy insight a minute ago has been transformed with a single twitchy digit into client relationship suicide. "I'll handle this one," I'd bragged to my own company's managers as I'd saddled up for Redmond. "Listen and learn," I'd insisted to rolling eyes.

What am I going to do now? What can I say? "Orlando, did my brother just send you an e-mail? He's back on the meds but I'm thinking that giving him my password wasn't such a great idea." By now it's almost 3:00 a.m. and I'm not thinking too clearly—although I'm real clear that I've got to get to Orlando before that e-mail gets to the entire Microsoft executive team as Introducing the Gospel According to Stan Slap. I call the front desk and ask for a wake-up call for 5:00 a.m. "That's only two hours from now, sir," the desk clerk informs me helpfully.

Meanwhile

Orlando is only hours away from leaving for the remote facility deep in the Oregon woods where Gates, Ballmer and the company's eighty top executives are gathered to plot global strategies in a meeting titled "Microsoft: Software Dynamo." Key to the plan is Orlando's presentation of sales opportunities. It's one of the first on the agenda.

Meanwhile

The hotel phone shrilly announces the wake-up call and I stumble back to the laptop. An hour later I've composed a fairly lame e-mail that informs Orlando that while I'm not taking anything back, one could, of course, read what I sent a couple of different ways—or, better yet, one could not read it at all. I move to send the e-mail, intentionally this time, and can't get online. *Aaargh!* Wireless isn't available in the hotel and I'm under the desk chiseling through the wall with a room service fork in search of frayed cords when I realize I have no time for this; I have a roomful of people waiting for me. I glance at the clock by the bedside and see that the phone next to it is off the cradle from my fumbling it after the wake-up call, and that's why I haven't been able to get online. I hurriedly send the second message to Orlando.

Meanwhile

Orlando has already begun his presentation—by announcing to the room, "I don't want to talk about sales. I want to talk about me. I want to talk about the fact that I can't be real in this company."

He is greeted by stunned, suspicious silence. This guy looks like Orlando. This guy sounds like Orlando. This guy is not Orlando.

"Let me tell you a little bit about myself, about where I come from and how I know what's real to me," Orlando gushes on, in full *Jerry Maguire* mode. "If I can't live my own deepest values at work, and if we can't be real to ourselves and to each other, then how are we ever going to be real to our customers?" he pleads.

Silence.

Orlando goes for the big close. "There isn't an empire in history that thought it was going to fall before it fell."

Silence. And the room explodes.

The eighty top managers in the company rise to give him a five-minute standing ovation. Everybody is lustily cheering—"I'm hurting, *too!*" Everybody except Bill Gates, who sits glaring stonily at him.

"You just did a very bad thing, Orlando," Gates says. "You just said we are bad people. We are not bad people."

"Bill," Orlando says, "if that's what you can say to me after your top eighty executives just gave me a standing ovation, I don't belong in this company," and starts to walk out.

"Wait a minute, wait a minute!" yells Ballmer.

Meanwhile

"I wonder how it's going with Orlando," I ponder idly, chewing a croissant during a break in my own morning's meeting.

Today

Eighteen-year Microsoft veteran and then senior vice president Pieter Knook managed one of the company's seven major business units. "I was in the *[Bury My Heart at Conference Room B]* meeting earlier that week so I knew what Orlando was trying to do. I just couldn't believe he was trying to do it *here*. We were searching for strategies to make more money and the guy in charge of worldwide sales was saying that we didn't even have a clear sense of why any of us were at the company, but he was sure it wasn't the strategy and it wasn't the money. It got very, very tense in that room."

"I was given an hour and a half for my talk," says Orlando. "It lasted twenty minutes. I said shame on us for putting ourselves in the position we're in, taking this kind of fire about our business practices and our integrity. We can't be different on the outside than we are as people on the inside. I said I personally feel my values are being compromised and I will not be part of that, no matter what."

"At first, Bill felt personally attacked, thinking what he had built in his company was being threatened. It was exactly the opposite," insists Knook. "It was an amazing moment, a positive impact on the entire executive staff of a large company. We decided we were going to spend all our time on this instead of the planned agenda since anything else seemed irrelevant at that point. From here was born the reincarnation of what we think the company is about and that it starts with us as human beings."

"I was very troubled the night before," admits Orlando. "I kept questioning why I suddenly felt compelled to say these things out loud. My answer was that you cannot wave a hand and say, 'Today I'm not but tomorrow I am.' Where do you draw the line? I had done a lot of thinking that week and I kept arriving at 'You can't escape from yourself.'"

He shakes his head. "Right before I started, I remember thinking, 'Let's see how real this company is.' The last thing I expected was the reaction I got. People were standing up and clapping and I didn't know what to do. There were people crying. It was the most bizarre thing I've ever seen.

"Where does the bond come from that creates common purpose?" he poses. "I agree that belief in a cause starts with believing in who you are as an individual. Every individual is capable of leaving a legacy," he says. "That legacy comes from being real at all times. The only person who can determine relevancy to yourself is you."

"How does it feel to do that?" I ask. Orlando's eyes begin to narrow with trademark intensity and . . .

He smiles deeply. "I feel liberated."

HOW TO SELL IT
TO YOURSELF

10

ANAGERS ENTERING THE *Bury My Heart at Conference Room B* process wrestle with this all the time: They see that there's a place they can take their jobs far beyond what they thought possible but don't want to move forward until they're sure they can sell the concept to themselves, their employees and their company. I can definitely explain how to sell it to your employees and your company, but I can only hope to convince you to sell it to yourself, which is where the sales chronology has to start. It's something only you can decide and it's more an issue of your confidence than your competence.

It may not be that easy to do at first. Think it feels funky when your foot falls asleep at work? Just wait until your heart starts to wake up. But what becomes wonderful most often begins as fearless. Once you really know what your values are, the bigger risk is not doing it.

"Why bother to live my values?" This is a question you should ask often—if your attorneys are planning an insanity defense. Contribution and community are what await you when you live your values. Your values will drive your unique impact on the world, whether it's for your own small family or the family of man.

Man is born to dream, to be enlightened, to connect and to be fulfilled. Managers are too. This is what it means to live your values at work and this is the decision that awaits you now. You are a leader if you change the world around you in the name of your values. This is it, stripped to its naked, glorious essence. Stripped to its naked, shivering essence, your job as a manager is therefore a perfect vehicle for leadership. Not only are your values under pressure—a legitimate reason for leadership—but you can use those values to improve the lives of others—a legitimate platform for leadership.

Getting people to support what you believe in most is the great triumph of leadership. Getting you to support what you believe in most is the great leap of faith. The strategies and tactics used by the greatest leaders in history have immaculate translation to your world as a manager. Can you use these to become a leader yourself and get the same impact? You can, but the first—the essential—step is to stop yourself from thinking you can't.

WHY JOHNNY CAN'T LEAD

You don't have to wheeze your way up the Himalayas to worship at the smelly feet of the world's one leadership guru; as of this writing, there are 380,687 titles in print about leadership—83,524 about "business leadership"—and U.S.-based Fortune 500 companies alone spend an estimated $12.3 billion each year on leadership development for their managers. You can get a bunch of information about leadership any time you want it, and surely you've had exposure to the concept even if a lot of that exposure was useless, generalized or wrong.

If you're so smart—and let's face it, you are—and you understand the importance of leadership—and let's face it, you do—then why aren't you doing all the things that leaders do—and let's face it, you're probably not. Here are the ten big myths that prevent a manager's natural transition to leadership. Let's bring 'em up and bust 'em down.

► 1. "I DON'T HAVE WHAT IT TAKES"

The problem with having great leaders as role models for your own development is that by the time they come to your attention they've already got their act together. You see them when they're larger than life, playing on the world stage and passionately delivering flawlessly constructed rhetoric to dewy-eyed masses.

You don't see them when they're starting out, desperately recruiting the first followers, stumbling through the initial construction of their vision ("I have a . . . *spleen.*" No, that's not right. "*We* have a spleen." No . . .), facing overwhelming odds and a power structure that is well resourced, dug in and disinclined to cede any territory.

Despite their humble beginnings, history's greatest leaders have racked up some pretty impressive accomplishments. How exactly did they achieve these results? If the concept of leadership is stripped of the mythology and manipulation that typically surrounds it, are there certain things great leaders always do—an A, B, C, D to leadership? Is there a reliable schematic to these things—an A + B + C = D? And even if there were both, why would anyone do it in the first place? Don't look around; you know who I mean by "anyone."

The original research for *Bury My Heart at Conference Room B* included a ten-year analysis of many of history's greatest leaders, across time spans, geographies, civilizations and disciplines, in search of answers to these questions. Enough suspense already: Found them. The ignition switch is an urgent desire to relieve pressure on their deepest values. The schematic is a series of tactical moves, often planned and performed in a certain order, to enlist the support of others.

There is no leadership school that can claim history's greatest leaders as alumni. They all started for a reason and figured it out. The same reason that will drive your own leadership.

A Leader Knows Exactly Who They Are
and Exactly Where They Want to Go

What first separates a leader from a normal human being? A leader knows who they are as a human being. They are acutely aware of what moves them; a leader has such self-awareness they could confidently name their most important values.

Most people don't know themselves that well. They may be driven by their most important values. They may be driven crazy by not living their most important values. That doesn't mean they know exactly what those values are. That doesn't mean they're making daily decisions to protect and promote what's truly most important to them.

Leaders are different and, because they know what's truly most important to them, they know what they want the world to look like—a reflection of what's most important to them. Example: Martin Luther King Jr. discovers that he's got core values of Freedom, Equality and Spirituality. He knows then what he wants his world to look like—calls it *"I have a dream."* The only problem? He can't make that dream happen all by himself; it's too big. He's got to turn his beliefs into irresistible, gripping beliefs for others. This is where and why leadership begins.

Leaders do great things for the world, but the initial motivator is that they want to meet their own deepest values. If a leader knew who they were, knew where they wanted to go, knew how to get there and could get there all by themselves, they'd just go. They'd send you a postcard from the Promised Land: *"I have a dream. You're not in it."*

Leaders Are Fabulous Communicators

A leader is never lazy about communication. They can't afford to be; every chance to communicate is another chance to sell or resell their leadership vision. They are always aggressive and always creative about communication—and always working to turn information into *meaning* for people. This is what makes leaders such compelling communicators. Even if you don't agree with them, you'll find yourself listening to and remembering their message.

A lot of people in positions of power today are big, well-dressed rich people. To look at some of history's greatest leaders, you wouldn't think they'd be as naturally commanding to an audience. Mohandas Gandhi was a short, barely dressed poor guy—hardly a prototypical media darling. He was always intentional and passionate in his communication, though, and that earned him the edge he needed to command attention.

A leader isn't charismatic because they have a big following—that would just make them a personality. They're charismatic because they're an extraordinarily centered human being. A leader is focused on and relentless about what they believe in—focused and relentless almost to the point of insanity. This intensity is translated to their communication style. If you'd been shackled to Gandhi for a few years, you'd have been mighty inspired. At first. Eventually, you'd have considering gnawing off your leg to get away. *Mo, please, I get it.*

Leaders Create the Highest Level of Trust

If you can't get people to trust you, they won't follow you anywhere. Trust? Uh-oh, you're thinking. *Trouble.* Not to worry: Establishing trust as a leader isn't exclusively about your personal moral character, and this is what makes it so dangerous in the wrong hands. Of course, it's nice if you happen to have some personal moral character, but you could conceivably be the same disco lizard you've always been and slither your way into a leadership position. As long as you earn a special kind of trust from your followers.

The trust that a leader most needs to establish is about commitment to improving the lives of their followers. That's why followers are signing up, and they'll make their decision to trust based largely on two criteria: consistency and passion. A leader is consistent—they do exactly what they say they're going to do, small things and big things. A leader is passionate—deeply, obviously emotional about what is most important to them.

Leaders don't just create trust; they create the highest level of trust possible amongst human beings: A leader creates faith. They have to create faith because they're promising to deliver you to a place that they've never been to themselves, that they can't get to without your help and that is going to be spectacular for you even though it's suspiciously based entirely on fulfilling *their* own values. In essence, a self-serving journey to be made in total darkness as fast as possible. Gee, what a sweet deal for the average follower.

Consistency and passion are more than just fundamental elements of trust; they help create a vital aura of competency. Competency can be a tricky issue for leaders because they often can't actually prove they can do what they say they can do. Fortunately, successful experience is only one aspect. Consistency, passion, commitment, focus, intensity and a clear vision of what's wrong and what's right are others, and a leader has all of those in abundance. Leaders create faith because they have faith in themselves.

Leaders Make a Lot of Mistakes

A leader makes more mistakes than a manager ever dreams of. *"That's it, I'm a leader!"* you're thinking. Sorry, it's not just screwing up that makes you a leader. It's what you do about it that counts.

While it's true that a leader makes a lot of mistakes, they don't make the same mistake over and over again. They're always moving on to new, far more glorious mistakes. That's because a leader learns from their mistakes. They learn from their mistakes because they admit them to themselves. They admit them to themselves because what a leader cares about is getting to a place where their values are fully realized. Any mistake that gives them information on how to get there faster is worth the mistake.

● ● ●

Of all the keynote speeches John Pepper gave as chairman of Procter & Gamble, it's the one about ethical business practices for the Society of Competitive Intelligence Professionals that he probably remembers most. Especially when two employees of a P&G contractor who were engaged in spying on the competition were subsequently arrested climbing out of the Dumpsters at Unilever headquarters, where they'd been sifting through the garbage for trade secrets.

His response? Directly contact the apoplectic president of Unilever to apologize and then insist P&G go public with the story, including his admission of total accountability. Granted, the mistake wasn't his own—he didn't meet with a couple of bozos in P&G ninja costumes to review battle plans: "I'll distract them with a speech while you hit the trash." But he is a man driven by deep personal values, integrity being one of them.

Years later, John was running the finance department at Yale, where campus security had no doubt been instructed to obsessively monitor activity around the trash cans. I asked him how long it took to decide what to do about the Unilever disaster. "Two seconds," he said dismissively. "It was easy," he added, swatting away my obvious next question. "Tough would have been to go home to my wife and my two boys and tell them that I didn't do what I knew in my heart to be right."

● ● ●

Leaders are equally fearless about admitting their mistakes to others; they know that no mistake they make is bigger than their vision and values. Want to know you're in the presence of a leader? Do these two things: 1) ask them about a mistake they've made, and 2) plan on having the whole day free. They'll tell you in exhausting detail about every embarrassing move they've ever made. Side by side, though, you'll hear the deep learning, the changes in behavior and the ever-increasing focus on getting to where they want to go.

Even more remarkable than making a bunch of mistakes and admitting them is that leaders actually encourage their followers to make mistakes. A leader knows that they don't have a chance of achieving their vision if they're the only one willing to take a risk to change the world.

● ● ●

Let us review: Leaders are people who know exactly who they are. They know exactly where they want to go. They're obsessed—hell-bent intent—on getting there. They're fabulous communicators, careful and creative, and always working to turn information into meaning. They create trust; beyond trust they create faith by doing exactly what they say they're going to—anything and everything—and by being obviously emotional about what's most important to them. They make a lot of mistakes but they admit those mistakes to themselves and change because of them, and they admit those mistakes to their people. And they encourage their people to make mistakes in the name of their vision and values.

Worried that leaders are rare superhuman beings and you'll never make the grade without somehow gaining the ethical foundation of Mother Teresa, the oratory power of Martin Luther King Jr., the events budget of Steve Jobs or the unwavering focus of Rex the Wonder Dog?

Leaders are indeed rare human beings. But they're just human beings, after all, and the things they do can be done by anyone—anyone who understands what's truly most important to them. Understand your own deepest values and you'll naturally be intense about communicating them to others, consistent in the things you do, clearly passionate about your beliefs, insanely focused, willing to take an objective view of anything that helps you get to a place you know in your soul is better than any place else, and relentless in inspiring the reluctant to help you do it.

▶ 2. "IT SEEMS LIKE A LOT OF SACRIFICE WITHOUT A LOT OF PAYOFF"

Most managers would rather be Jack Welch than Lech Walesa, and who could blame them? The perks package sure seems sweeter and, putting nobility on its own special shelf in the back where it will be safe, it's a whole lot more, uh, *efficient* to do good things for others from the top down, rather than struggling at the bottom and working up. Besides, by any measure, many of the world's most renowned leaders have suffered in the name of their leadership.

By any measure but one: fulfillment of their core values. No one could deny, for example, Nelson Mandela's remarkable sacrifice for his deep beliefs. But at least he *knew* his deep beliefs and was focused on realizing them. Leadership taps into energy and conviction that is simply unavailable to most people. History's greatest leaders were and are the most soul-satisfied human beings on the planet.

Mukhtar Bibi. Stephen Biko. Benazir Bhutto. Julius Caesar. César Chávez. Winston Churchill. Crazy Horse. Indira Gandhi. Betty Friedan. Mikhail Gorbachev. Václav Havel. Aung San Suu Kyi. Abraham Lincoln. Napoleon I. Oscar Romero. Anwar al-Sadat. Malcolm X. Viktor Yushchenko. It probably hasn't escaped your notice that many of history's accomplished leaders either were shot, beaten severely, hounded from their community, spent nearly a lifetime in jail or toiled in wretched poverty. Can you be a leader without enduring these unpleasant side effects?

Sure: I'm going to sneak you in a side door marked *Tactical*.

You want to call yourself a leader? You don't want to call yourself a leader? What's important is that you learn to do those things that leaders do so you can get the benefits that only leaders get. Leadership will connect you to your most important personal values and turn your cause into the common cause, but there are plenty of other benefits, and they'll all be yours when you apply leadership in an organizational environment.

Your People Will Follow You

Your people won't just follow you to the successful completion of a project or financial objectives, although they'll follow you there too. They'll follow you anywhere you point them to. Imagine a world where your employees would care about what matters most to you as a human being and devote themselves to helping you live it. If you're waiting for that to happen to you as a manager, forget it. Nobody will ever line up behind you as a manager except maybe to push you down the stairs.

Your People Will Listen to You

Hearing happens when audio waves trigger the nerve endings in the inner ear, creating an electromagnetic pulse that's decoded by the cerebral cortex; you will cause this as a manager. Listening happens when people are motivated to understand, remember and care about what they've just heard; you will cause this as a leader. Your people don't listen to you as a manager; they wait for you to stop talking, which isn't quite the same thing. Imagine a world where what you say synchs up, not sinks down.

Your People Will Have Faith in You

You need to create faith in your employees since you couldn't explain the wisdom behind many of the things you ask them to do if your life depended on it. Imagine a world in which your people believe in you as a human being, not simply as a manager. A world in which they'll support you even if they don't always agree or understand. A world where they have faith that, although all you ever seem to talk about is your own values, those values have a distinct benefit for them.

Your People Will Grow with You

You're going to grow; leaders are people whose careers accelerate in any organization because they truly understand how to achieve results through others and they work with a confidence and purpose managers never dream of. Your people are going to grow too. Imagine a world where, no matter where they go in work or in life, they'll say to themselves and to others that they were never more convinced of their personal potential than when they worked for you and that it's your role model of authority they practice in their own lives. If you've ever wanted to leave a lifetime legacy in the hearts of others, or simply wanted to turn ordinary working relationships into cultlike worship, this is the way. Leaders change the world. You're going to change your own world and you're going to change theirs.

▶ 3. "I'M CONFUSING MANAGEMENT AND LEADERSHIP"

It's easy to do. The word "leadership" is slung recklessly about, casually attributed as adjective, verb, noun and pronoun, often abused and misused. In fact, authentic leadership is hard to find in the two environments where it's most often self-proclaimed: politics and business. It is followers who keep a leader in place. When the primary purpose of leadership isn't to serve that true constituency, the leadership is fundamentally corrupt.

Politics is all about compromise—the constant spin and sound bite. It's hard to get elected if you've ever made a mistake or taken a passionate position about anything. In real leadership, mistakes are a healthy part of the process. And while real leaders may be tactically wily, they don't compromise their values.

Business is all about compensation—the constant promotions and options. These motivations would leave history's greatest leaders snortingly unmoved—is that *all* there is?

There are plenty of real leaders in business; they're just not always the people who are called leaders. They may be leaders or they may be superb managers, which is not necessarily the same thing. No one is a leader by position alone. No one has leadership vision just because they have a smart go-to-market strategy. No one has followers just because they have headcount.

Social history's greatest leaders have often been judged by time, which means they created a legacy of impact that survives long beyond their tenure. Their motives were pure—not always right but always what they said they were—and they were remarkably resistant to sway from temptation or stress. In the light of increasing renown, they remained empathetic, aware and involved in the world of their followers. Anyone who applies this kind of real leadership to industry will make history.

Leadership is different from management in the type of results it produces, and for this reason it's more important. Management controls performance in people because it impacts skill; it's a matter of monitoring, analyzing and directing. Leadership *creates* performance in people because it impacts willingness; it's a matter of modeling, inspiring and reinforcing. How can you control what you haven't yet created?

The relative quality of performance from your people has little to do with their skill. They already know how to do their jobs—you hired them because they had that basic capability and, once they get an orientation to your products and procedures, they're competent. From that point on, the quality and quantity of their performance depends on their willingness to use their skill to the utmost, regardless of whether you're hovering over them like some supervisory gargoyle.

It's wasted effort attempting to get more skill from already skilled people by focusing on impacting their skill. Leadership will achieve short-term results and it will create an environment where long-term goals can be reached more dependably. Leadership affects how you get there, not how long it takes to get there.

Consider all the things that managers have gotten people to do in the 3,500 years of recorded business history. Pretty amazing—unless you stack it next to all the things that leaders have gotten people to do in that same amount of time. The relationship between leaders and followers is humanity at its most potent and profound. Humans will give it up for leaders in a way they'll never give it up for managers.

Actual leadership is counterintuitive to a lot of the things you learn, witness and are reinforced for as a manager. Most of the things you do as a manager will be management things, even though they'll often be called leadership things. Most of the people you work for will be managers, even though they may call themselves leaders. Most of the companies you work for will misuse the concept of leadership, even though they'll use it constantly. In fact, there is a profound difference between leadership and management. Here's the short form:

No matter how eloquently or expensively delivered, whether it's via e-mail on the small screen or at an off-site on the big screen, every management message is an equation that ends only one way:

$$= \text{Work harder.}$$

Every leadership message is an equation that also ends only one way:

$$= \text{Live better.}$$

If your people don't believe they're going to live better by working harder, they won't work harder. Of course, the same goes for you. That's what we're doing here.

▶ 4. "MY COMPANY WON'T BUY IT"

Social history abounds with examples of simple people who've moved millions to stunning acts of devotion without any position of power other than what was granted to them by followers. None of these people were managers; they probably couldn't have held on to a corporate supervisory job if their lives depended on it. On the other hand, they did "manage" to gain all the attention they needed, refashion the world in the name of their operating values and strategic vision, inspire rabid support from followers during the toughest times and leverage almost nonexistent resources for a magnificent return. Be glad Mother Teresa isn't helming your competition—she'd smoke ya.

They all did it by being able to create emotional commitment in others. Their abilities in this area are as well known as the leaders themselves, and finding out more about them is but a bookstore away.

Getting Abe Lincoln to deliver the keynote at your next executive off-site is tough, but getting the principles of his leadership conveyed to those attending is easy.

I once casually mentioned to Charles Schwab that he'd nailed the blend of management and leadership pretty well—and the conversation immediately stopped being casual. His response was fast and emphatic: "I don't care how smart you are, how great you are. The most important thing is to allow yourself to be as open and fragile as everyone else. Then you become a real person and there's never, ever anything wrong with that."

"You *go*, Chuck," you're thinking. "But what if my own mystery dance bears a disturbing resemblance to Disco Night at the Toledo Elks Club? Will my company buy my initially clumsy transition to leadership? Will my company ultimately buy my authentic leadership behavior?"

Maybe not, but it doesn't matter. What your company will buy is any reasonable action that produces business results, and real leadership will definitely produce business results. Most companies are superstitious about results and about the people responsible for creating them; the more demanding the company, the more it will be supportive of any action that causes action.

Your job as a manager requires achieving results through others. Leadership is the single best method to do that. As long as your vision doesn't violate the basic objectives and principles of your organization, those results will be hard for anyone to argue with.

Managers are forced to eat from a magic plate: No matter how much you swallow, nothing ever seems to disappear. It may be hard to conceive that your company will allow you the time to adopt new behaviors and practices, but hold on to this: Leadership will buy you that time. It will cause you to give more of a commitment and gain you more commitment and protection from your team.

Worst case? Nothing in your company changes but you. That will be enough.

▶ 5. "MY COMPANY HAS DIFFERENT VALUES THAN I DO"

Companies are generally more concerned about performance than behavior. Manager behavior is important as a driver of allegiance and productivity, but it's not about fulfillment for its own sake, or feelings, for God's sake. Corporate "values" therefore tend toward the likes of Accomplishment, Power, Loyalty and Security, whereas managers' values tend toward the likes of Family, Integrity, Creativity and Health.

This is the crazy-making conflict between management trying to act on behalf of the company, which is comprised of managers trying to act on behalf of themselves. The needs of the collective always being more important than the needs of the individual makes a lot of sense. Unless you're the individual.

From the company's perspective, the values of managers, which are based on contentment, can seem to challenge the values of the organization, which are based on performance:

- You have Family as a value? We don't want you thinking about being unable to spend more time with your real family.
- You have Integrity as a value? We may need you to represent a product or policy you don't believe in.
- You have Creativity as a value? This is the way it needs to be done.
- You have Health as a value? Sometimes we need you to work harder than is healthy.

In a values smack-down it would seem like your company, with all its resources and methods of influence, would be favored to win. But managers have their own leverage—emotional detachment—which can bring a great house down or drive it to distraction. There is a seemingly built-in, intractable tension between the two perspectives, and the only guarantee is that nobody wins unless it is resolved.

It won't be resolved without some mutual respect. For you this means respecting that you are seeking fulfillment in a hosted environment. Freedom to pursue your values comes with responsibility to protect the company's values. For your company, this means understanding that its position as landlord doesn't grant it the right to enter managers' hearts at will and rearrange things to suit it.

A lot of the friction between values of the enterprise and those of its managers can be defused with understanding that the best chance of both sides getting what they want is by both giving the other what it wants. As with so many things, it all comes down to safety. The company has to feel safe that managers are devoted to meeting corporate values so it will allow them the opportunity to meet their own. Managers have to feel safe that they can meet personal values so they'll put effort into the company's version. It's a shared accountability before it's a shared satisfaction.

Fulfillment of a corporate value such as Power depends on managers applying personal power. If it means giving up their own to do it, that's going to produce false power, undependable in the clutch. A company can't just require its managers to obey. Today's marketplace battles require that they think. To do this without reservation means they first have to feel—feel in control according to their own values.

What this control gives you as a manager is not freedom to pursue your own priorities regardless of the company's, which would be nuts, but freedom to bring your true self to work, which would be great.

▶ 6. "MY PEOPLE WON'T BUY IT"

Won't buy it? *Won't buy it?* Let me toss you the slop bucket of enlightenment as you wallow in your naïveté:

Your people are dying for your leadership. If they're not buying it, it's only because you don't yet know how to sell it to them. Your people want and need the humanity, inspiration, purpose, direction, confidence and unity that leadership gives. Oftentimes, your biggest initial cynics will become your biggest supporters. They've backed off because they've looked for leadership and been let down before they ever met you. They may be disgusted but they're not disinterested.

You might still be thinking of history's greatest leaders. Give you a global threat or national class struggles and you'll come storming out in the full leadership outfit. But as a manager? Where's the burning platform?

Many people often live without values satisfaction, their own or common ones they can believe in and depend on. They regularly sacrifice what is truly most important to them, sometimes to get ahead, sometimes just to avoid falling behind. Your people also work in a world that moves fast and changes constantly. It's a world where they face regular reminders of how little control they have over the events that affect much of their daily lives.

This *is* life during wartime.

Your leadership will give them something to believe in. In a world that has become increasingly cold and empty, your leadership will provide warmth and fulfillment. In a world where the threat of change is constant, your leadership will provide something to hold on to. If leadership and what it offers is increasingly tough to find anywhere else in their world, how important is yours going to be?

▶ 7. "ISN'T BEING A MANAGER ENOUGH?"

Do your job, do everybody else's job and now add Chief Evangelical Officer to the job description. Just what you needed: *more* work. What if you just want to be a manager?

As a manager, you already have to devote constant energy to motivating your people. Leadership is going to make that a whole lot easier to do and a whole lot more rewarding for you. Maybe you just signed up to be a manager, but you can't be maximally successful as a manager without being a leader. You can't be maximally fulfilled, either.

You have a job as a manager and it's to protect and promote your company's values, just as it's your job to help realize your company's vision of world domination. Simultaneously, you have an opportunity as a leader, which is to protect and promote your own values and make your own vision happen. Leaping on your opportunity as a leader won't hurt your job as a manager. It will protect it.

The myth of management is that your personal values are irrelevant or inappropriate at work. This is absurd—where do your values *go* when you're on the job? Leadership allows you to incorporate your personal values into your work and to gain constant support for those values from those around you.

When you're a manager, you work for your company. When you're a leader, your company works for you.

▶ 8. "I CAN'T ALWAYS PROTECT MY VALUES AT WORK, SO HOW CAN I ADVOCATE THEM TO OTHERS?"

It's reasonable that you may have distanced yourself emotionally from your people after realizing you could be forced to leave them someday or be forced to make them leave you—it's hard to talk about behaving like a family to some while saying to others, "We're reorganizing and you're out of the family. Good luck finding a new one; drop on by to let us know how you're doing. Not at dinnertime." Advocating values of Security, Health, Creativity, Learning and others when you can't guarantee them is enough to give anyone pause. Certainly anyone with Intelligence as a value.

As a manager, your options for resolving such conflicts may not seem that attractive. Withdrawing from normal relationships with your people because they hold you responsible for their welfare in an uncertain environment poses a problem: You can't get real results from false contact. Besides, you need them to help you live your values on the job.

As a leader, though, you have a fine-looking alternative:

Bring your team together, fire 'em up with emotional commitment and you'll be amazed at what they can do to relieve the pressure on your values in all sorts of real-world situations—common purpose doesn't extinguish in crisis; it emerges. Their inspired productivity will go a long way in allowing you to protect them. If anyone ever has to leave, your humane leadership will have made a lasting impression on what people can expect from themselves and from those in positions of authority.

Leaders are extraordinarily capable of selling their vision—transforming, subverting and navigating past opposing points of view. The fundamental skill of leadership is the ability to unite others in common purpose. You're only in this alone because you haven't started it yet.

Should you leave your company if your values are under steady fire? If circumstances are truly dire and hopeless, and you've already tried to apply these methods, that might be your best option. But remember that things change in organizations, this may be the best job you'll ever have and no job may be any different. Better to take your stand where you are, make it better for you and your people, and drag your company right along with you.

When you embed the meaning of your values within your team and convince people to protect them—which I'm going to show you how to do starting in a few pages—you'll have a good chance of realizing them at work and so will they. They'll create this ability for you as much as you will for them. The impact on the business that results will give you air cover to keep it going. You may not be able to control everything you have to do as a manager, but you can control a lot of how you do it.

▶ 9. "MY PEOPLE HAVE DIFFERENT VALUES THAN I DO"

Leaders don't care about somebody else's values as much as they care about their own. They may think it's nice that you have your individual values, but that doesn't necessarily have a lot to do with their leadership.

Check out that whole seventeen-minute speech: Martin Luther King Jr. clearly said, "I have a dream." Eight times. He did not say, "Of course, that's just my dream. I'm sure you have your own dreams. So now we're going to break into separate Dream Teams and come back together with one big dream statement!" He was saying, "*My* dream. *My. Dream.* But what I'm going to do is use my dream to make your lives better than you ever thought possible so it will become your dream too."

In this same way, you must stay selfish. If the fulfillment of your values isn't first a personal motivation, you won't be driven to complete the new behaviors required to become a leader, which means you won't be able to provide the benefits of leadership to others. Without this you won't have the skill to incorporate their values too—you've got to build a sustained working model in the surest way possible. You can help your people in the search for fulfillment of their own values at work, and you should—but only after you've learned how to do it yourself. For now, the key words in the phrase "my own values" are "my" and "own."

Don't be concerned about whether your employees have different values. They'll still support yours if yours have positive impact for them. It's not like any combination of values you picked as your top three could be punishing to them. What? As if your people don't have enough problems? Now their manager has swallowed some twisted new business book without chewing and they're forced to have fun, be healthy and live in integrity? *"Hellooo, HR!"*

▶ 10. "I DON'T HAVE ANY ROLE MODELS"

If you had been surrounded by leaders your whole life—if, by some miracle, your parents, extended family, teachers, first manager and elected officials had all been role models—you would know how good it feels to follow a leader. When you became a manager and had the potential to lead, it would be natural for you to attempt to create that feeling in others. Even if you didn't know exactly how to do it, you could reverse-engineer enough of what had been done to you to get started.

Chances are that you weren't and aren't surrounded by these sterling examples. To live in today's world is to be constantly confronted by breaches of leadership at the highest levels. Politics, business, religion, law enforcement, charity—pick any category on any day and some morally dyslexic officeholder will be only too happy to justify your lack of faith.

Here's what you need to know most about leadership: Lead your own life first. The only thing in this world that will dependably happen from the top down is the digging of your grave. You're waiting for leadership to happen *to* you? Leadership happens to you as soon as you understand your own values and understand how to enroll others in supporting them. Instead of waiting for a leader you can believe in, try this: Become a leader you can believe in. The sooner you start to practice leadership, the sooner your personal values will start to be realized. So what exactly are you waiting for?

Unless Procrastination is one of your big personal values.

HOW TO SELL IT
TO YOUR PEOPLE

11

HERE HAD TO be a catch somewhere. Living your values at work requires the support of others. If the people around you care, you've got a chance of achieving this for over half your waking hours. If they don't, you won't.

The process starts with getting people's attention in a way that makes them believe your values are even worth considering.

There are three ways to get your people's attention.

The first way is bribery. One problem: Doesn't work. The carrot may achieve short-term results, but it won't inspire the honest, sustained effort a leader needs. The successful leadership battle is fought for your people's hearts, not their pockets.

Leaders don't use bribery. The Dalai Lama's team is lucky to get souvenir bars of motel soap when he returns from another triumphant world tour. Sure, the soap is blessed, but still . . .

All is not lost, for there's another pair of nose pliers in every manager's tool kit. The second way is fear. One problem: Doesn't work. The stick may achieve short-term results, but it's the longer-term result you have to be concerned about since anger is the natural psychological reaction to fear. Inspiring a constant level of hostility among your people is a seriously flawed strategy. They may be smaller than you are, but there are a whole lot more of them; you're a lamb chop in the piranha bowl.

Leaders don't use fear. Imagine Mother Teresa snarling, "You've just sponge-bathed your last leper in *this* town, little sister!"

Historically, leaders didn't use the carrot and they didn't use the stick. They didn't have the carrot and the stick. Yet they got people to do things you can't get them to do, and you do have the carrot and stick. How is this possible?

The third way to get your people's attention (Hint: THIS IS IT) is with your hand, in which you symbolically reach out that hand to your people. "Grab hold," you are saying, "and I'll take you to a Better Place."

You're thinking, "Let me get this straight: I should call my people together, leap on the desk, thrust out my hand and plead, 'Take my hand and I'll take you to a Better Place.' Yeah, *that's* going to happen *real soon*. You don't know my people. If I hold my hand out, they'll put something nasty in it. Or maybe they'll take a finger off. Besides, I joined my company for the options package, not to be the spiritual guiding light of my organization. I'm not going to do this. It's a stupid, embarrassing thing to do."

I agree with you; this is a stupid, embarrassing thing to do. I'm not recommending that you do it.

Unless.

Unless by at least metaphorically saying to your people, "I can see a Better Place. Take my hand, let me take you there," you could get your people to say to you, "This Better Place—this is a place based upon the fulfillment of *your* deepest personal values? That's why you want *my* help? To get you to a place where your values are fully met?"

"All right. Let's go."

This would be the best ROI you'll get from any hand gesture made to your people. Which might be why every leader in history has done exactly the same thing to begin achieving amazing results.

STEP ONE: DEFINE THE BETTER PLACE

In leader-speak the Better Place is called "vision." Because their vision is driven by true belief, leaders really can see that Better Place. You may not yet see that Better Place for yourself or others, but it exists as surely as, and because, your values exist.

Seeing it yourself isn't enough; your people have to see it too. Leaders create vivid descriptions of this Better Place. They have to describe it so you can really see it. Why? Because no one really can see it—it isn't here yet. It won't be real until people help the leader make it real. And so a leader describes what life will be like in this Better Place in as much rich detail as possible. You don't just see it when a leader describes their Better Place—you can taste it.

▶ ONE SMALL STEP FOR A MANDELA, ONE GIANT LEAP FOR MANAGERS

If you were a world leader, your leadership would be taking place on the world stage and your promise of a Better Place would be improved global conditions in the name of your values. As a manager, the stage you're playing on is your own work organization, and the conditions you are changing in the name of your values are working conditions for your people. If you manage the entire company, the company is your organization, but if you manage a team, the team is your organization, not the entire company.*

Your definition of a Better Place is what life looks like with your values fully realized. The definition of a Better Place for your employees is vastly improved working conditions based on your values. You can't get to this Better Place by yourself; leaders have to expand their vision to

---

* Not yet, anyway.

realize it. Make the promise of the Better Place clear and credible to your people and they'll help you get there.

Grab the highlighter: You don't actually have to explain how you're going to get to this Better Place. Leaders rarely do, and it's not because they're confusing coquettish with charismatic. It's because they don't have a clue about how to get there. If they knew how to get there, what would they need you for? They only know that they must get there and so they must get you to want to get there too.

Accurately defining it is just the first step—a declaration of intention—but it's an important one. The Better Place isn't a gift to your people; you need their help to get there. Unless you're very clear about what "there" looks like, the help won't be offered.

Building your vision of a Better Place starts with a deeper under-standing of what your values really mean to you. What makes them your top three values? Beyond the literal definitions of the words, what do these values *give* you that causes them to be so important?

If you picked Family as a value, it doesn't simply mean that you love your partner, children or parents. Look beyond this to what those relationships provide that is of such high personal priority. Is "family" a place where you are assured of unconditional support, open and honest communication, and when you need it, tough love? Is it a place that you can always go home to, where you can stumble and fall and still be forgiven, where you can rage on about your passions and be listened to without judgment? Is it a place where you are surrounded by people who often put your welfare ahead of their own, inspiring you to do the same for them?

▶ THE VALUE OF TRANSFERABLE CURRENCY

This definition of meaning is what makes family vital to you, and you shouldn't have to put it aside when you're at work. You don't have to: The definition of why it's so important to you is also the key to getting your people to support the same meaning. This is the *transferable currency* you can use to define the Better Place for them, in the name of your values. Welcome to the first step any leader takes to convert their values into a compelling cause for others.

Fear not: Insisting on the value of Family as a defining characteristic of how people will be treated isn't advocating that your people get to leave at noon every day to spend naptime with their preschoolers or join you at home every Friday for Team Spaghetti Night. It means that the definition of what Family—or any of your most important values—means to you will be understood, enforced and protected by all.

"Unconditional support," "open and honest communication," "listened to without judgment," "tough love," "stumble and fall but still be forgiven" and the rest may be your own definition of fulfillment, but they also happen to be fabulous working conditions, of benefit to any employee. These are definitions of your values that translate immaculately to the promise of a Better Place for others. What's most important to you becomes most important to your people, and in order to get it themselves they have to deliver for you. Tell me you're not loving this.

The ultimate importance of any value is that living it allows you to feel safe, confident and inspired. This is your Better Place and your people are going to want to go to that Better Place; they'd have to be crazy not to. In order to get there, they have to drag your values right along with them. They have to manifest the very behaviors you are describing and they have to create the very conditions in which they want to live. If they want open and honest communication, they're going to have to be open and honest in their communication. If they want unconditional support, they're going to have to support each other unconditionally.

And they will. They just need the focus, the sanction and the deep commitment from you. They need your help to "see" the Better Place. As soon as they see it and decide they want it, their movement forward will create the spark that ignites your leadership. Martin Luther King Jr. didn't make his dream happen—the 250,000 people in the audience on August 28, 1963, and the millions those people later inspired, willingly took on that job. You don't have to get yourself to the Better Place; you have to get your people to want to get there.

If you have five people on your team, that's now 500 percent more horsepower aimed at getting to your Better Place. If you have fifty people, that's now 5,000 percent more horsepower. If you have five hundred people, hang on: You're strapped tight to a herd of hungry, nostril-twitching thoroughbreds that has just sensed far better grazing potential over the next big hill.

Your vision does have to be somewhat grounded in reality; it's only inspirational on a sustained basis if people believe it can be achieved. History's greatest leaders were so sure of the correctness and importance of their values, they believed they could change the world—it wasn't an unrealistic goal for them. Likewise, your vision of a Better Place can be a stretch. Maybe a real stretch. But a stretch in this lifetime.

▶ STOP SAYING WHAT YOU WANT THEM TO HEAR

Your vision of a Better Place should not directly be a financial one. Your Better Place isn't about market share; it's about what your team shares. It's not about customers, financial goals or anything else pointed outside. It's about the quality of working conditions based upon achievement of your values. It's pointed inside.

Financial success—for your company, for you or for your people—is one of the effects of leadership, but it's not a cause of leadership. "To increase sales" or "to gain higher productivity" are solid management goals, but they're not leadership vision destinations. As blasphemous as it may seem, words like "competition," "customer, products," "quality" and "revenue" don't belong in any description of your Better Place. The idea isn't to arrive at your destination financially satiated and emotionally ravenous.

Don't worry about the financial part—leadership is the first and best way of delivering on any corporate financial objective. Instead of focusing on how the business results are going to happen, focus on getting your people to want those results to happen for their own deepest reasons. Automatic reminder notice: If your people believe they're going to live better by working harder, they'll work harder.

Would the people who work for you be able to pick your top three values immediately and unhesitatingly from a long list? Would they be able to describe your Better Place in compelling detail? If the answer to either of these questions is no—and for most managers that's the answer to both—then you haven't begun to see anything of the performance your people are capable of.

MY VALUE: Family

Say to Yourself

What It Gives Me That Makes It So Important:
- Unconditional support
- Open, honest communication
- Honest feedback
- Support if I make a mistake
- Involvement in and contribution to the lives of others
- Protection if something goes wrong
- Feeling good—reasons to celebrate

Say to Your People

Let Me Take You to a Better Place:
"This will be a place where you will never again put your job and your family into conflict without giving me the chance to do something about it. Your job and your family will be strangers no more; you're doing good, important work here, and as we celebrate that for you, we're going to roll that celebration right out to your family—the people who make it possible for you to get in here every day and do that good work. When you have something great going on at home, I don't want you to have to leave it locked up at home; you roll it in here and we will cheer you on. Know this: If something ever seriously goes wrong at home, you will have the strength and support of this family during your hard time.

"Because we're family here too; we're together all the time, so it's time we started acting like a family. I mean the very best of families: This team will have open, honest communication. This team will have unconditional support. When we need it, this team will have tough love, but if you ever stumble, this team will help pick you up. Under pressure, this team will never turn on this team. Instead, this team will come together to protect this team because that's what families do and family is very important to me."

• • •

MY VALUE: Integrity

Say to Yourself

What It Gives Me That Makes It So Important:
- Safety, knowing that I can depend on the accuracy of the information around me
- Respect, knowing that how I see the world is accepted even if it's not agreed with and that I can speak the truth as I see it
- Growth, knowing that I can safely learn and practice new behaviors

Say to Your People

Let Me Take You to a Better Place:
"This will be a place of integrity. You will be able to make decisions safely because you'll be able to depend on the information coming to you as being the truth, the whole truth and the truth on time. If I ever can't tell you the truth in this way, I'll tell you the truth about *that*. This will also be a place of respect. We will respect the truth as you see it even if it's not the popular truth. This will be a place where it is going to be all right to be accountable. You can try things if you believe in them, you can admit if it didn't work out as planned and you can learn from it. You will have the chance to grow every minute of every day.

"This will be a place of safety. This will be a place of respect. This will be a place of growth. Because this will be a place of integrity and integrity is very important to me. This will be a place where the truth lives and the truth will set us free."

MY VALUE: Spirituality

I'm going to use spirituality as a third example here because companies often blanch at the legal liability and potential for abuse if managers are allowed to advocate theirs at work. That's understandable, but when used as a leadership method—the transferable currency of their beliefs—spirituality is neither a religious argument nor an insistence on one correct ideology. It's the positive impact for their team based on any manager's definition of how spirituality can improve working conditions.

There's no threat to the enterprise here. Even if a company believes solely in financial fundamentalism, letting managers bring the transferable meaning of their values to work is the pathway to revenue salvation.

Say to Yourself

What It Really Gives Me:
- Belief in a higher purpose
- Respect for all living things
- Moral compass
- Inner peace
- Something I can lean on
- Connects me to the world

Say to Your People

Let Me Take You to a Better Place:
"This will be a place that means something to us all. Not just for the work we do but for how and why we do it. You'll find a foundation of strength and peace in this: We're going to do business the right way—ethically, with respect for everyone we deal with inside and outside of this organization. We will never lose that sense of what's right despite any pressure or temptation to compromise.

"We're going to step up to execute the work that comes our way, but we're also going to leverage the fine minds and fierce hearts that are this team for a greater purpose than just the day-to-day effort. What is that purpose? I don't yet know but I know this: We're going to find it and we're going to find it together. When we find it we will find peace in this place."

• • •

SO CLOSE. SO FAR AWAY.

true tales from the *bury my heart* files

Iin Nugroho is her company's human resources manager for Indonesia. An exceptional calm surrounds this woman, like wisps of a cloud, and on this day it spreads softly but surely to envelop the room, amplifying her presence. In that room, full of coworkers and those who work for her, she is explaining where her value of Determination comes from.

■　　■　　■

"I was almost six years old. One morning I woke up and tried to get out of bed and I fell on the floor. I could not move my left arm and my left leg was numb. When it didn't go away after several days my father took me to his friend who was a doctor in one of the biggest hospitals in Jakarta. When this doctor saw me he immediately said, 'She's getting polio.' We went home and my father was crying and then my mother was crying, 'What did we do wrong?'

"So that's how I got that and what happened.

"Polio was very new and not many people understood it. The doctor had two options for my parents. He will give me some medicines to make sure that it will not spread to other parts of my body, except then I cannot move my left arm and my leg forever. He gave my parents another option that was still experimental.

"He believed he could affect the nerves with a different temperature. The only way to do it is with water because you cannot change the temperature of the air that quickly and dramatically. My mother and my father decided they would take this option, although it is not guaranteed to work and requires a great sacrifice from them: They will have to see me in pain and they will have to cause the pain.

"The procedure is that every three hours I have to be put in scalding water, for one hour. Every three hours, every day, twenty-four hours a day. My mother has to measure it on her hand, which is more thick-skinned than the rest of the body, and if it is too hot for her then it is the right temperature. Boiling water. Oh!

"I am sleeping and my mother would wake me up and then put me in the hot water. I didn't know the scientific reasons. I didn't know anything and my parents didn't want to tell me. I was just a little girl and I didn't understand what was happening to me. I didn't know I was sick. They put me in this big metal tub, like a pail, with high sides. When I was inside, I cannot get out by myself because it is so deep and the water is up to my neck. I was so scared. It is so hot; it is so painful.

"My mother always brought me to the water as quickly as possible because it had to be very hot. My father tried to help by bringing my small toys to cheer me up but I couldn't hold on to them. My mother picked me up and held me after but I always feel like, 'How could they do that?' I am just crying and crying and crying.

"The doctor kept saying if I could move a finger at some point that is good. Then if I can move some more fingers and hold this little toy then we will let you wait four hours between the water, not three. So I put this encouragement in my mind; and I feel really, really good because he showed me I can do something about it, he gave me something, a goal. And I did it. Every three hours became every six hours and then, almost a year later, the doctor gave me one more goal: I had to move my arm like I was pointing to something, which he said was the hardest part.

"And when there was a day when I could point to something, like straight pointing from my shoulder, then the doctor told me, 'I'm done here. You are cured. You don't have to do the hot water anymore. And I remember he was crying. And I was so happy at that time I did not even cry, I was just thinking, 'No more hot water.' And I was looking at my arm and saying, 'I can move it now!'

"Even today I cannot stand hot water. When I take a shower I have to turn all the heat on in the house, then run into a cold shower and run out.

"What this taught me as a little girl is that if you try to do small measures, at the end you can achieve a big thing. It is sometimes painful but at the end you will be there. When I was in the horrible water, I always think, okay, it is a small step you need. If you fail, try to do it again or do it differently. But do it. Do smaller steps because at the end you will be there.

"I feel like if I didn't go through that experience, I would not be able to be like I am now. Everything I have today is from there, where I am strong and patient and trust myself and don't give up. Try it again, try it again, I always tell myself.

"We live in a fast-paced world where everybody is eager to achieve the best in everything. This is good, but there is nothing wrong in starting with a smaller achievement and then going to the next level. Let's talk about your problem. We can always solve it. We will both think our way through it."

Ignoring the tears in her eyes, Iin smiles. She seems to check within herself that her point has been made. She nods. Done.

Not done.

The guy sitting next to her rears back, aghast. "Oh, no. How could this be? I have worked for you for so many years. Whenever I bring you a big idea you keep stopping me, saying, 'Small steps, let's take small steps.' I have been so angry and frustrated all the time. I never knew. I never knew you. I worked right next to you and I never even knew you. I am so ashamed."

She looks at him kindly.

"I didn't realize it myself until just now. I know the experience I had but I didn't recognize how it has shaped my life. I didn't know that it would be useful for others. A lot of things have started making sense to me too."

▶ HOW TO DO IT

1. Decide the Greater Meaning of Each of Your Top Three Values

Move beyond the literal or common definition of the values words to what the values give you that makes them so personally vital.

2. Take Work Out of the Equation for Now

What do these values give you in your life overall?

3. Push Hard for the Ultimate Meaning

It's not the processes implied by the value; it's what those processes *give* you in life that makes the value so important. Strip each value layer by layer until you believe you've found the biggest benefits.

- If, to you, Integrity means telling the truth, what does telling the truth *give* you that makes it so important in life? If telling the truth to others means they'll feel comfortable telling the truth to you, what does *that* give you?

- If, to you, Health means avoiding stress, what does avoiding stress *give* you that makes it so important in life? If it means you have more energy to do what you want to do, what does *that* give you? If it gives you the opportunity to do more things, what does *that* give you?

- If, to you, Accomplishment means doing a lot of things and doing them well, what does doing a lot of things well *give* you? If it gives you confidence that you can meet any challenge that comes your way, what does *that* give you? If it gives you the chance to experience things you would never have otherwise been able to, what does *that* give you?

4. Combine the Benefit Descriptions of Your Top Three Values

This will give you the definition of your Better Place.

5. Connect Their Better Place with Yours

Your promise of a Better Place for your people should also be an accurate description of a Better Place for yourself. If you could walk into work every day confident that you would be able to live in this Better Place, would that mean you're actually living these values to their fullest benefit? You should be able to draw a straight line between the meaning of your values and your description of the Better Place.

STEP TWO: BACK THE BETTER WITH THE BITTER

If there is one thing a leader is great at, it's inspiring you with a vision of a Better Place. A wonderful destination, tantalizingly out of reach but realizable by joining his righteous crusade. A place more beautiful than you can ever imagine without his help.

If there's another thing a leader is great at, it's making you absolutely miserable by describing how much your life sucks right now because you're not in that Better Place. You're in a place even worse than you could ever imagine without their help.

To encourage you to dream of a Better Place, leaders have to be very clear about the nightmare of your current reality. They create urgency and momentum by creating conflict between where you are now and where they want you to go. They use every motivational lever available to get your attention: If their promise of splashing around in the lake at Camp Paradise doesn't motivate you, they'll point out that your house is on fire. Now, won't that water feel good?

It's not fair to ascribe this all to tactics; leaders believe that a world without their values fully realized is a world gone wrong for all. You'll gain the same acute perception about the state of things in your organization when you begin to look at them through a filter of your own values. You'll see what others may not and you'll be compelled to call it out to them.

Leaders will talk about the *Bitter Place* almost as often as the Better Place. Managers, on the other hand, avoid talking about how bad things are. This generally isn't due as much to company loyalty as to fear that people will riot if they realize it. What a grand scam: As if your people, who are regularly experiencing these conditions, wouldn't know it if it wasn't pointed out by their manager. Leaders are aware of the suffering of their people; you will earn valuable empathy points when you describe the Bitter Place in excruciating detail.

Mostly managers hate to talk about tough things because they can't do anything to change a lot of them. As a leader, you're not leaving your people in this bad place; you've got something else to offer them and it's something rare and beautiful.

You've got the promise of a Better Place.

The Better Place is a description of future working conditions based upon the meaning of your values. The Bitter Place is the current unsatisfactory state of what these values mean to you as experienced every day with your team.

If one of your core values is Learning, are people in your organization completely open to the viewpoints of others from inside and out, responsible but reinforced for their own regular learning and supported by policies that advocate constant new experience and education and the transmitting of knowledge throughout the team? If one of your core values is Adventure, are people in your organization safe to explore the new and untried, able to act counterintuitively, free to take their own road to a required corporate conclusion and allowed to tweak the mundane to make it a bold experience?

If everything is fine, then leave it or give them an idea of what it would look like if it wasn't fine, wasn't constantly protected by all. Don't make up miserable conditions if they don't exist—even if Creativity is one of your values. But chances are that things aren't as good as they could be. Chances are that you haven't yet communicated your values to people, that you haven't yet translated those values into a promise of better working conditions and that you haven't yet enrolled your people in a passionate effort to make those conditions happen.

Chances are that the state of your values isn't what it should be, for you or for them.

If that's the case—if the working conditions are often tough, exhausting, stressful, unfulfilling and in direct violation of what you believe in most—*tell it like it is.* (This is my own first rule of management: Sanction the Inevitable. If things suck anyway, claim it's part of your well-conceived strategic plan.)

Say to Yourself

I Have Family as a Value:
- Unconditional support
- Open, honest communication
- Honest feedback
- Support if I make a mistake
- Involvement in and contribution to the lives of others
- Protection if something goes wrong
- Feeling good—reasons to celebrate

Say to Your People

This Far, No Further:
"We're not acting like a family that any of us would want to be part of. We don't support one another. Everybody's under pressure, and instead of looking out for each other we're looking for ways to gain an edge on each other. We don't talk, we don't listen—we don't really communicate at all. If you stumble and fall, you're going to stay on the

ground until you can pick yourself up, and nobody's going to risk their own position to help you. We don't share anything about ourselves; it's as if no one has any personal circumstances or passions. It's not like this is helping anybody. By everybody protecting themselves it's become a threatening place for us all."

Say to Yourself

I Have Integrity as a Value:
- Safety, knowing that I can depend on the accuracy of the information around me
- Respect, knowing that how I see the world is accepted even if it's not agreed with and that I can speak the truth as I see it
- Growth, knowing that I can safely learn and practice new behaviors

Say to Your People

This Far, No Further:
"We accept all the pressures on us to deviate from what we know to be the best way for our organization to serve the company and then we consider ourselves victims of forces beyond our control. We separate personal from professional integrity when we know that there's really no difference. This isn't a safe place to learn or grow because it's not a safe place to make a mistake. We consider the truth an option, not a requirement, and dwell in shades of grey when it comes to telling the truth to us or to others.

"When we rationalize not telling the truth, we knowingly send false information into the universe. People make decisions based on that information and those decisions are wrong because we've caused them to be wrong. Those decisions come back as information to us and our decisions are then wrong too. And what are we saying to someone when we withhold the truth? You don't deserve the truth, or you're too stupid to realize you're being lied to. When we show such disrespect to others we disrespect ourselves in equal measure. When we force our people to hide their mistakes we force them to hide from the important lessons those mistakes can give. We remove our own accountability and we remove the inclination of others to tell us the truth.

"The worst part of the way we're treating the truth is, I fear, that we're not fooling anyone, inside our team or on the outside."

Say to Yourself

I Have Spirituality as a Value:
- Belief in a higher purpose
- Respect for all living things
- Moral compass
- Inner peace
- Something I can lean on
- Connects me to the world

Say to Your People

This Far, No Further:
"There is no real meaning to the work we do; all we do is get it done over and over again. We show no respect for others—we roll our eyes if they can't keep up with the pace and talk about them behind their backs. There is constant anxiety in the team because we haven't taken a stand on the right way to do business and we let the agendas and priorities of others decide that for us. There is no greater point here, and our achievements are hollow because of it. All of these fine minds and hearts gather together every day and yet we have no connectivity to any higher purpose. It's not just that we've compromised our beliefs; we're not even sure of what those beliefs are."

► HOW TO DO IT

1. Describe Any Current Dissatisfactory State of Life on Your Team

Use any ongoing violations of your values as the criteria for the description—the meaning of your values (transferable currency), not the literal definitions.

. . .

2. Pull No Punches

You should *not* be okay with these conditions because they are a continuing violation of your values. The stronger your message here, the more vivid the difference will be between the Better Place and the Bitter Place. The more credibility you'll earn for it being important to you and for your awareness of what conditions are like for your people.

BUZZING ABOUT THE COMPANY PICNIC
true tales from the *bury my heart* files

I'm in a large meeting room with three levels of managers—entry, middle and senior—reporting to one another. Senior managers are in the front, entry in the back, middle in the middle.

"No problems. Everything is good here!" comes the resistance, as it often does from managers when asked to describe the Bitter Place. Especially when their own manager is in the room with them.

"How can that be if your people can't even name your values and couldn't even describe the *Better Place*?" I ask.

"It just *is*," comes the emphatic reply. "We're fine."

"How can that be if your people can't even name your values and couldn't even describe the Better Place?" I ask again.

"Even if it weren't okay, I wouldn't go out of my way to talk about it," interrupts an exec VP from the front row. "I don't think it's the right thing to do. It's unprofessional and it won't inspire anyone."

"That's right!" insists the back of the room.

"It's the pathway to real inspiration," I explain. "It's important to build credibility by showing that you are not okay with any violation of your values."

"Maybe it is tough at times," the VP finally admits. "There's a lot of stress and not much work/life balance, but we're in a competitive market and we've got to hit our numbers. We can take it," she adds proudly. "We thrive on pressure here and we thrive on change—we suck it up and move on."

"Suck it up! Move on!" from the back of the room.

"Let's take a break for a while and I'd like you to reconsider this," I urge her. "The Bitter Place isn't whining and it isn't pessimism. It's about confronting reality to make reality better and that's always the right thing to do."

"Want to try again?" I ask when we return. She sighs, and then nods determinedly, stands and faces the room.

"We are like flies, feasting on week-old mayonnaise, left rotting in the sun," she declares.

Huh. That's progress, I think to myself.

"Well, okay then; it's time to move past that Bitter Place," I say. "Let me show you how to use this tough situation to motivate your people to change it. Now, the first step is—"

"*Month*-old mayonnaise!" come numerous mutterings from the back of the room.

STEP THREE: GIVE THEM SOMETHING FOR THE TRIP

The good news is that you have just described the beautiful pot at the end of the rainbow for your people. The bad news is that between where you are now and where you want to go are forty miles of bad road called "Real Life at This Company." Paint whatever sunny picture you want—if your team's weather report calls for howling winds and blinding rains along the way, they're staying home.

Your people are all too aware of how difficult it's going to be to get to your Better Place. And let us not forget that you haven't exactly been to that Better Place yourself and come back with souvenirs for everyone. You're asking your people to walk down a hard, long, risky and, worst of all, unproven road. You can't just promise them a spectacular conclusion; you've got to give them something spectacular along the way to keep them moving. Yes, it's one of those wretched journey-is-the-destination moments.

History's greatest leaders have always faced this same problem: It's not enough for your people to want to go there; they have to be willing to *get* there. Leaders solve the problem by giving their people the ability to get what they want most with every step they take toward the Better Place. This keeps them in self-propelled forward motion.

What is it that your people want most?

As good a motivational model as any to understand this comes from Abraham Maslow. We'll use his, since every great leader has intuitively used something just like it and since most managers vaguely remember waking up in a puddle of drool in some business class and hearing his name before passing out in another puddle of drool. Here's what you missed in between:

Abraham Maslow was a pioneer in humanistic psychology and organizational development, first hitting his stride in the forties and peaking in the sixties. His efforts have since been proven many times to be credible, as opposed to some of the things you may have done during that latter period. Essentially, Maslow said that human beings are "perpetually wanting" animals. What motivates people to action is what they want most.

Big deal, you're thinking, my kid could do that kind of research. That's it? No, that's not it. Maslow also found that all humans want the same things. Since we're wanting animals, as soon as we get those things, we move on to the next things we want. In a fit of reckless creativity Maslow called this order the "hierarchy of needs."

The natural first priority of any living thing is to survive. So it is with humans, and this forms the first level on the hierarchy of needs. Survival includes air and it includes procreation (see: "perpetually wanting animals"), but on a day-to-day basis is mostly about food and shelter. Pursuing the satisfaction of these survival needs is why we humans do what we do. At least until we meet them, at which point we promptly stop caring about them and move on to whatever's next on the list. This next move is critical because once physical safety needs are met, what humans hunger for most is emotional fulfillment:

The need to feel *significant:* Who I am and what I do matters in the world.

The need to *belong:* I am an accepted and protected member of a tribe.

The need to feel *self-worth:* I am a good person doing good things.

One difference between base physical needs and higher psychological needs is that the human ego rarely gets enough of the second kind. You can stuff yourself with emotional fulfillment until it's dribbling down your chin and your ego will quickly chomp it down and demand more. Try it: No matter how smoothly you're breezing through any given day, you'll be reluctant to confidently proclaim, "Hey, no more positive self-worth for me, pal. Give that compliment to some homeless guy who needs it more than I do."

The impact of this for you as a manager is considerable: An employee's primary safety needs are already met because they're employed. They have regular incomes, which produces confidence that they can feed and shelter themselves. They may not be able to live in the fabulous style to which they believe you're accustomed, but worst case, they can sign up for a bunch of training sessions to nab some extra food and grab whatever secure sleep they need in meetings.

The impact of this for you as a leader is crucial: History's great leaders didn't have a choice about whether to use the promise of emotional fulfillment; they didn't have any money to give. Even if you have the money to give it won't work—the greater commitment you need means the promise of fulfillment has to be greater too. It has to be emotional fulfillment, and it's these feelings of significance, self-worth and belonging that a leader delivers to their people.

Or rather that a leader causes people to deliver to themselves. The key is not to keep pushing the buttons that move your people forward; it's to cause your people to push their own buttons. This is how leaders extend their deep reach without constant direct involvement with their followers. They don't just use a motivational method; they use a self-motivational method. One that allows people to feel emotionally fulfilled with each step they take toward the Better Place.

Once human beings have been fed and let into the house, the primary motivation for their behavior is emotional fulfillment. When you can show them how to get it by helping you get to the Better Place, better leap to the side of the road or they'll flatten you in the rush to get there.

Stairway to Heaven: Maslow also said that if you were one of those rare individuals who had safety needs regularly met and knew they always would be, and had emotional needs regularly met and knew they always would be, you would climb the hierarchy of needs all the way to *self-actualization*. This level is as sweet as it gets in life and is achieved by few. Self-actualization comes from knowing who you are and the way you want your world to be, and being able to cause that to happen. This is the life of a leader.

This is the tactic of a leader too. They'll explain that getting to the Better Place is important, which means you're important for making it happen—you are *significant* as you help get the team there. While we're at it, it takes a special team to get to the Better Place and you're part of that team, working together to achieve something urgent and valuable. You *belong* as you help them get there. Oh, and one more thing: It isn't easy getting to the Better Place. You have to be smart, tough, dedicated, focused and the best at what you do. You have *self-worth* as you help them get there.

Keep in mind that, as with all motivational methods used by leaders, this one must bear up under a bothersome standard: It has to be legitimate. You're asking for a faith-driven effort from the employee culture, which will instantly sniff out whether you're sincere. The advantage of promising emotional fulfillment for movement toward your Better Place is that it happens to be the truth. It *is* important because it ensures a better quality of life for them, it *does* take a special team to make it happen because you can't do it by yourself, and it *isn't* going to be easy so it's going to require personal character they can be proud of.

You will have engaged your people at an entirely new level. Once they believe that arriving at the Better Place will be good for them but the act of getting there will be too, you'll have triggered their amygdala's attention. Remember, this is the driver for the limbic system, the part of the brain that makes decisions.

The limbic system is also the source for humans to be affiliative, which means (a) all humans are hardwired at the factory to want to support a cause, and (b) the humans who work for you will react supportively when they gain the sense of common purpose that the push toward your Better Place provides. Strangely, pointing out that it's not going to be easy to get to the Better Place will move them forward too. Just the potential to generate positive neurochemicals causes the brain to create more of them. Go figure.

You don't have to remember all of this brain code stuff. You just have to remember that causing your people to feel emotional fulfillment along the way to your Better Place will energize them and make them instinctively act in whatever way creates more of the same good feeling. You might also want to remember that if they *don't* feel this, they'll curl up in the back of your leadership wagon with a supportive

"Wake me when we get there, Chief."

Your leadership isn't a gift to your people. You need their help to get to the Better Place, and they're going to have to do some work to get there with you. A leader doesn't deny this effort required of others; they make it maximally fulfilling.

Want to feel that you're significant, that you belong and that you're worthy? Keep moving to that Better Place. If Pavlov had figured out this dependable ring-your-own-bell method, he would be known for the global franchise, not the interesting experiment.

Say to Your People

Family:

SIGNIFICANCE

"This is so important to us because we can't take care of our family outside the job unless we behave like a family right here. When we do, we'll have open, honest communication and unconditional support, and we'll be able to depend on each other when things get tough."

BELONGING

"It's going to take a team and not just any team. I can't do this by myself—I need a group of special people that perform like a family."

SELF-WORTH

"It isn't going to be easy. We're going to have to be dedicated and focused. We're going to have to be the kind of people who watch one another's backs. We're going to have to be strong enough so that nobody can break apart our commitment to mutual success."

Say to Your People

Integrity:

SIGNIFICANCE

"This is so important to us because sooner or later we have to go home and look at somebody. Maybe it's our partner, maybe it's our children or maybe it's the mirror. How did we stand up to the pressures to compromise our integrity? At the end of any day, quarter or project, what do we have but our own good name?"

BELONGING

"It's going to take a team and not just any team. Integrity happens because a group of special people decides that they're going to make it happen."

SELF-WORTH

"It isn't going to be easy. We have a lot of pressure on us to shade, withhold and deny the truth. That's okay; we're the kind of people who are strong enough to hold up against it. We're smart and we're brave and we know how to protect the difference between right and wrong."

Say to Your People

Spirituality:

SIGNIFICANCE

"This is so important to us because we're here for a reason and that reason can be as meaningful or meaningless as we want to make it. It's important because the respect we show to all people inside and outside of this organization determines the respect they show to us."

BELONGING

"How are we going to do it? It's going to take a team and not just any team. It's going to take this team of extraordinarily competent and connected people."

SELF-WORTH

"It's not going to be easy. A lot of the meaning of our job is decided by others. We're going to have to be strong enough to find it anyway. We're going to have to be smart enough to figure out how we want to work and unshakeable enough to not be pushed off that platform."

· · ·

▶ HOW TO DO IT

1. Link Your Better Place with Their Significance

Your people become more important by doing something important. Show them why getting to the Better Place is important—not just to them but also to the entire team.

Significance: "This is so important to us because . . ."

2. Link Your Better Place with Their Belonging

Your people belong if it takes a team to get to the Better Place. Show them why it takes a special team working together to achieve something so unusual and important.

Belonging: "This is going to take a team and not just any team . . ."

3. Link Your Better Place with Their Self-Worth

Your people become more worthy if it isn't easy getting to the Better Place. Show them why they must be competent, tough, committed, focused—the best at what they do—to reach the Better Place.

Self-worth: "This isn't going to be easy, but this is who we are . . ."

STEP FOUR: CONNECT IT UP

What does it look like when all the steps are put together? It looks like you've got something that's different, sensible and compelling.

▶ 1. MY VALUES

Start with the understanding of what is most important to you.

▶ 2. THE BITTER PLACE

Using what's most important to you as a filter, describe the unsatisfactory conditions affecting your team.

▶ 3. THE BETTER PLACE

Again using what's most important to you, describe how good life can be for your team.

▶ 4. SOMETHING FOR THE TRIP

Translate their support into fulfillment by showing how their support confirms their significance, belonging and self-worth.

That's what it looks like. Here's what it sounds like:

▶ "THESE ARE MY DEEPEST PERSONAL VALUES"

"I believe in many things but these values are most important to me: Family, which gives me unconditional support, open and honest communication, and contribution to the lives of others. Integrity, which means I can trust the information given to me, there is respect for the truth as I see it and I have the ability to learn from my attempts and grow from my mistakes. Spirituality, which gives me a moral compass, inner peace and respect for all living things.

"This is what I've learned about living. I refuse to do without the benefits of these values at work, a place I spend over half my waking hours, and I refuse to have people I care about do without them either."

▶ "THIS IS HOW WE ARE LIVING NOW"

"We are not getting the benefits of these values today. We don't always support one another. Everybody's under pressure and instead of looking out for one another we're looking for ways to gain an edge on each other. We don't talk, we don't listen—we don't really communicate at all.

"We accept all the pressures on us to deviate from what we know to be the best way to serve the company, and then we consider ourselves victims of forces beyond our control. This isn't a safe place to learn or grow because it's not a safe place to make a mistake.

"There is constant anxiety in the team because we haven't taken a stand on the right way to do business and we let the agendas and priorities of others decide that for us. We're not even sure what we stand for as the people who make up this team."

▶ "THIS IS HOW WE ARE GOING TO LIVE"

"This will be a place of integrity. You will be able to make decisions safely because you'll be able to depend on the information coming to you as being the truth, the whole truth and the truth on time. We will respect the truth as you see it even if it's not the popular truth. This will be a place where it is going to be all right to be accountable. You can try things if you believe in them, you can admit if it didn't work out as planned and you can learn from it. You will have the chance to grow every minute of every day.

"This team will have open, honest communication. Under pressure, this team will never turn on this team. Instead, this team will come together to protect this team.

"We're going to do business the right way—ethically, with respect for everyone we deal with inside and outside of this organization. We will never lose that sense of what's right despite any pressure or temptation to compromise. We're not only going to execute the work that comes our way, we're also going to leverage the fine minds and fierce hearts here for a greater purpose than just the day-to-day effort.

"Family, Integrity, Spirituality. How are we going to make these things work together in this company, with all that we have to do? I don't know that but I do know this: It's exactly what we're going to do."

▶ "THIS IS WHY IT'S SO IMPORTANT"

"We can't take care of our family outside the job unless we behave like a family right here. When we do, we'll have open, honest communication and unconditional support, and we'll be able to depend on each other if things get tough.

"The respect we show to all people inside and outside of this organization is going to determine the respect they show to us. At the end of the day, the question is, how did we maintain our personal integrity amidst the pressures that surrounded us? We're here for a reason and that reason can be as meaningful as we want to make it."

▶ "THIS IS WHY IT TAKES A SPECIAL TEAM"

"How are we going to do it? It's going to take a team and not just any team. It's going to take this team of extraordinarily competent and connected people."

▶ "THIS IS WHO WE'RE GOING TO HAVE TO BE"

"It's not going to be easy. We'll have to be the kind of people that watch one another's backs. We're going to have to be tough and focused so that nobody can break apart our commitment to mutual success.

"We need to be smart enough to figure out how we want to work and strong enough not to be stopped from getting there. Things can get crazy around here. Fine—we're going to be crazier than that in our dedication to what we know is right: We'll be brave and impossible to stop."

● ● ●

You don't need to know how to make your values happen at work; you need to know how to get your people to want them to happen. This is what you have now begun to do by transforming what is most important to you into something of importance to them. How are your people going to avoid staying in the Bitter Place you've just described and move to the Better Place you've just sanctioned? By dragging the meaning of your values right along with them. What's in it for them along the way? Fulfillment of deep emotional drivers.

You are going to get noticed when you offer them this package. There are still steps to go to activate your leadership, but like the song says, you've found a driver and that's a start.

HOW TO SELL IT TO YOUR COMPANY

12

D o you doubt that your company will endorse the provocative concepts this book advocates? My two decades of experience implementing this solution in many of the most demanding companies—companies that don't include "patience" on their list of corporate values—shows that it will. As long as performance is increased while risk isn't.

Those companies that are most intense in their drive for performance get most warm and squishy—maternally protective—about any new way of achieving better results.

You can gain enterprise support for the prioritization of your personal values when you can translate it into business impact. To do that, you've first got to translate it into skill. Here is how to do both.

STEP ONE: SOLVE OLD PROBLEMS IN A NEW WAY

Companies that prize competency the most often don't slow down long enough for it to develop. In these get-it-done environments there isn't a lot of room to incorporate deep learning or to experiment with new behaviors, and there's not a lot of tolerance for failure.

"Emotional commitment," "your core values," "the Better and Bitter places." You've been armed with some bold new ideas and urged to walk the plank in front of your company to try them out. You may suspect these ideas roughly translate to "Hand me that saw, Alfredo."

Hopefully you now have the willingness to adopt the principles of *Bury My Heart at Conference Room B,* but how do you safely turn them into skills without practice? They need to be integrated into your regular management job in a way that helps you become more successful. That way you'll have a reason to use them regularly until they become reliable tools. Our purpose here is not to build a vacation home; it's to serve you where you really live.

Under constant pressure to perform, the last thing someone will chance is the counterintuitive move. You'll reach for what works, even if you know it doesn't always work. This is how to apply your values and your leadership promise to issues likely to occur in your world. Reach for this instead.

► HOW TO DO IT

1. "I'm Entering Q1"

You want to start the year right with everyone fully energized and focused:

SET CONTEXT FOR THE YEAR AHEAD

Remind your people that it's not just what they get done but how they do it that has meaning. Review the year's goals through the filter of your values with the team: Where will stress and temptation to compromise come from and how can the team defend against it? This is a chance to reaffirm their significance, belonging and self-worth. Ask the team to look back on the year and describe how they would have wanted to come through it—they can begin to write the story now so it ends the way they want it to—this is a reminder of the Bitter and Better places. Inform them that it's not just another year; it's another chance to define how they live at work.

SET CONTEXT WITH THOSE ABOVE

If last year was good for your organization, remind your own manager that it was affected by how you applied your personal values and legitimate leadership—reinforce the support they gave you then and lock it in for another year now. If last year was tough and troubled, explain how this one's going to be different because of the application of your personal values and legitimate leadership. Get their support for this better way of achieving results.

LOOK FOR OPPORTUNITIES TO CREATE LEGENDS

Let's look on the bright side: Opportunities will present themselves for you to prove you really mean what you say when you talk about your values and the Better Place. Granted, some of these, uh, opportunities will present themselves as maximum stress, upwardly ratcheting performance goals and previously unimaginable crises, but from an employee culture's perspective how you stay the course under pressure is the ultimate proof point.

2. "I'm Entering Q4"

You want maximum performance as you approach the point of no return:

REMIND THEM WHY RESULTS ARE IMPORTANT

Remind your team that this is no time to abandon the way they've chosen to work—it's going to get them the best results and a story to look back on that was written the way they wanted it to be written—not just what they did but how they chose to do it.

• • •

CELEBRATE EVERY RESULT ACHIEVED WITH VALUES INTACT

Stroke 'em and stoke 'em—every opportunity to reinforce performance done the right way—in support of your values and progress toward the Better Place—is important as you reach the finish line. Remember to be passionate—a little nuts—in response to their accurate efforts.

IF THINGS ARE WOBBLY, STEADY YOURSELF FIRST

If your team has historically met its annual or Q4 goals but is having problems this quarter, look to your own leadership. Have you consistently modeled your own values on the team? Have you been protecting and promoting the move toward a Better Place for all? If not, gather your people together now and reinforce it. Apologize if you feel there has been any default, recommit to them and start to prove it all over again. Be an overt example during this critical time.

SET CONTEXT WITH THOSE ABOVE

Everyone may be under unusual pressure as the enterprise heads into the final quarter. Make sure your own manager knows that you have performance foremost in mind in the way you have chosen to manage your people. You don't want your leadership derailed at this time because it's seen as inconsistent with the need for a full focus on results.

3. "I Need to Manage a Reduction in Force"

You want to get through one of the most unpleasant management circumstances with limited damage to your team and yourself:

REACT TO THE THREAT IN THE NAME OF YOUR VALUES

Key here is to protect your leadership credibility within the culture, even when you've shown yourself unable to prevent the loss of jobs. The best way to do that is by reacting to a threat to your values in the name of your values—act according to those values and to your leadership to begin limiting further damage and rebuilding the culture's peace of mind. As an example, if you have Health as a value, ensure that you are taking overt, exaggerated steps to let people talk through their anxiety and take care of themselves physically. If you have Creativity as a value, involve your team in developing innovative ways to make the RIF experience as smooth as possible for those being let go.

DON'T DISMISS THE IMPACT ON THE CULTURE

Your employee culture is going to be left shaken and self-protective by the RIF; just because the bullet missed them doesn't mean they won't feel wounded. When you need the most unity and focus from those who are left, it'll be harder to get. Trying to dismiss their concerns too quickly or too lightly will only exacerbate the problem and increase the divide between you and them.

You'll have a lot of questions about safety that you can't answer. Be honest with them about that—and committed to protecting them however you can. Remind them that their best chance is still found in working in a way that protects the team's ability to stay together and advance toward the Better Place. Honesty, empathy and conviction are what is needed now. These are the qualities possessed by every true leader.

HONOR THE DEPARTED

In order to gain the most from those who are left, you have to give to those who are leaving. If people simply disappear without their memory being honored, then they never really belonged to anything special in the first place. Instead, treat the people who are leaving with the same values as if they were still on your team. Keep them at least somewhat connected to the team, bring back news to the team of their success in finding a new job, pick a date on the calendar and get back in touch with general good wishes from the whole team. If you can officially help them with their trying circumstance, help them. If you can't officially help them, help them any way you can.

GUARD AGAINST YOUR OWN DETACHMENT

It's not as traumatic as being the one to lose their job, but an RIF can cause you problems as you administer it. You may not agree with the necessity or the way it's mandated that you carry it out; if this conflicts with your values, emotional detachment is a natural reaction. A hesitancy to promote your own leadership based on values you can't protect to people you can't protect is reasonable, but it won't get you anywhere. Your own detachment is harmful to you since leadership is about living your values at work, and it's dangerous to your people since leadership is about using those values to make life better for them.

4. "I Need to Reinforce Performance in a New Way"

You want to get maximum impact from performance reinforcement and you may have minimal resources to get it:

FOCUS ON WHAT YOUR LEADERSHIP PROVIDES

Take every opportunity to reinforce the meaning of your values, the sense of common cause, the opportunity to work in a values-based environment and the significance, self-worth and belonging that come from moving to a Better Place. You're not promoting yourself; you're promoting the benefits of what your leadership provides. This is what money can't buy.

CELEBRATE HOW THEY DID IT, EVEN IF THEY DIDN'T DO IT

Go ahead and celebrate your team's performance. Then raise the bar and announce an even bigger, better celebration because of how they performed. Make sure they understand what they would have missed if they hadn't delivered the results in a way that also supported your values and advanced the team to a Better Place.

EXPLAIN THAT THE BEST CHANCE OF GETTING REWARDED IS TO WORK ACCORDING TO YOUR VALUES

When your team is committed to protecting the way they want to work, they perform better. This is the best chance they have of delivering the results that earn material rewards and getting the deeper rewards that money can't buy.

5. "I Need to Get My Team/My Project Back on Track"

You want your people's extra creativity and effort to course-correct a plan in trouble:

LOOK TO YOUR OWN LEADERSHIP

If a project got off track in your organization, it's possibly because your people let it get off track. This is a matter of choosing to not use their discretionary effort. People work because they're inspired to—or don't because they're not. Have you been consistent in the application of your leadership? Have you reinforced your team's efforts to reach the Better Place?

LET YOUR VALUES BE THE ROAD BACK

Your original leadership declaration translated the meaning of values into the promise of improved working conditions for your people. It's those values that will help you restore any lost leadership credibility. As an example, if Family is a value, make it clear to them that your team acts like a great family when it's in crisis—no blaming, common goals, safe to be accountable, protect the family first. The translation of your values into benefits for your team is as valid as it ever was; let them now gain those benefits by putting the project back on track.

GIVE THEM A CAUSE WORTH PROTECTING

Get your people together and look at how poor performance has been allowed to violate values of benefit to them all. Give them a cause more meaningful than the project may be: Protect the organization.

6. "I Need to Recruit Top Talent in a Competitive Market"

You want the best people attracted to your organization:

GIVE THEM WHAT THEY CAN'T EASILY GET

Don't be undervaluing what you can offer to tempt top talent. Compensation is anything that motivates an employee. Inspiration, purpose, direction, humanity, faith, common cause, confidence and self-fulfillment can only come from working in a legitimate leader-driven environment. These benefits are rare in the world; in the world of work they're rarer still.

Money, job description, location—sometimes you can't compete with better offers when it comes to these components. Compete on your own field instead: Money and the rest are every company's commodity components of compensation. Your personal leadership and what that means to the quality of life belongs to you. They may be considering working for your company but they'll be living in your organization.

CHECK THE INVENTORY BEFORE YOU PUT IT ON SALE

The first rule of successful advertising: Don't say something until you stand for something. Before you start offering the benefits of your leadership, make sure they exist.

TALK ABOUT IT IN THE RECRUITMENT PROCESS

Explain what they can expect working in your organization: the intentional and constant effort to create working conditions with certain characteristics. Give examples of what this is like in the real life of the team—how it colors accomplishment, relationships, reinforcement, support. Explain that such a team breeds commitment and talent and the people in it get recognized for it. Talk about your values, talk about the Better Place, give them the Moment of Truth story—make sure they never forget this interview and can't wait to tell someone close to them about it. Ruin them completely for any other interview they may be having during their job search.

MODEL YOUR VALUES IN THE INTERVIEW

This will add credibility to your claims. If you have Creativity as a value, don't ask standard insipid interview questions. If you have Fun as a value, don't make the interview a Cold War interrogation from the other side of a desk. If you have Respect as a value, don't check your e-mail during the interview. (If you have Spirituality as a value, don't conduct the interview on your knees.)

ENCOURAGE THEM TO TALK TO YOUR PEOPLE

Insist that candidates talk to your people and encourage them to question what life is really like on your team—the priority placed on values and the impact on every person. Your people are going to answer by telling stories about you. You'll know this is happening because the fur will suddenly stand up on the back of your neck. The stories will either support your leadership claims or not and there is nothing you can do about it at this late date. Well, you can wrap your desk in aluminum foil to ward off the rays, but it doesn't always work.

STEP TWO: BENCH THE METRICS THAT MATTER

Unlike humans, business metrics never take time off. If metrics were human they'd have values of Accomplishment, Accomplishment and Accomplishment. If they were human they'd eat raw meat.

The key to protecting your individual implementation of *Bury My Heart at Conference Room B* is also using it to positively impact the performance measurements your company considers most important.

You're in good shape if doing that requires your own emotional commitment and discretionary effort; performance reinforcement for your people when traditional methods are unavailable or devalued; their increased unity of purpose, tolerance for change and faith in you when the circumstances of the company are in doubt. These are the metrics enhancement tools that have now been placed in your hands.

▶ HOW TO DO IT

1. Go with What You Know

The more comfortable you become in using the *Bury My Heart at Conference Room B* process the more opportunities you'll create for original business impact—stories to tell about assets newly leveraged and problems averted or resolved. But for now, don't try to reinvent what gets attention; stick with the metrics you're currently responsible for. This will make life easier for you, make the focus more understandable to your team and make the results more relevant to your company.

Depending on your position, metrics could include:

- Sales and margins
- Organizational health indicators
- Recruitment and retention of top talent

- Customer satisfaction
- Project completion

Performance improvement in any of these categories will be affected by your increased protection of the business as a result of being able to apply personal values to the work environment. The desire of your people to keep you delivering on the promise of a Better Place will cause them to deliver on team goals. Employee engagement and job satisfaction measured by any probable criteria is certain to be affected, and this will affect your ability to attract top talent. Customer engagement that requires your people to endorse the organization with their own good names will be influenced by the refreshed meaning the organization has to them.

2. Bench Them Right Away

Mark the present state of these metrics so you can continue to monitor improvement you can achieve no other way.

3. Use Them as Indicators with Your Team

Monitor performance improvement in these areas as a pragmatic indicator of people's growing faith in your leadership. If you don't see improvement, look to yourself first: Have you delivered on your promise to help them improve working conditions in the name of your values? Make any discussion about the metrics—good or bad—a discussion of team perceptions around this issue.

4. Measure in Rapid but Realistic Time Frames

Your business will have its own critical calendar and your initial ability to impact metrics through this process may not initially be in synch. But it's going to catch up soon and it'll be hard for anyone to catch you from then on. Check quarterly for the first year.

Some of your results may initially be anecdotal, but as any survey wonk will tell you, this is often the most telling, and patterns are easy to discern if you have enough of them.

STEP THREE: TALK IT UP

Sooner or later you'll need to perform a miracle in the name of your leadership—be allowed to reach a goal your own way, stop or slow a change, grant someone on the team special recognition. That decision won't be made by you but by someone a level or two above. You don't want to wait until that moment to explain that your leadership credibility hangs in the balance. If you'll need their support sooner or later, best to get it sooner. Grease the tracks ahead of time.

It's not enough to show the improved performance. Your company may have seen the results but not the new relationships—between you and your values and you and your team—that produced them. You need to continually explain how you got it, how you have increased your own commitment from material to emotional and how you have gained an entirely new level of commitment from your people.

Concerned about possible reaction? Chances are good that the levels above you will be far more receptive than you may fear. They are human beings and managers too; as such, they're sure to be struggling with the same issues of balancing personal values and professional responsibilities. If they have inclinations toward leadership themselves, they'll be naturally supportive of yours. They may be taken by your passionate declaration of values—leadership works up as well as down.

It's also likely they'll be interested in your tactics for applying the process and intrigued with the performance implications for their own world. Every manager has their own manager; even your CEO has a board, shareholders or outside analysts to answer to. Mother Teresa's supervisor—the person who did her performance reviews—was the Pope. Your boss just *thinks* they're the Pope.

► HOW TO DO IT

1. Make the Connection to Performance

Explain that the output of this process includes improved business performance—you're not planning on compromising results for fulfillment but just the opposite. Emphasize the cause-and-effect relationship between work harder and live better. When explaining your values make sure to note that it's not the literal definition of the words—Family, Creativity, Freedom, etc.—but the transfer of those words to better working conditions for your people.

2. Relate to Specifics

Relate this new process to a recent or historic organizational challenge—one that both you and your manager would know about. Discuss how leadership could have better resolved it. Even better, relate it to a current or upcoming challenge.

3. Be Realistic about Results

The results you promise may indeed be coming, but not all at once and not all tomorrow. Be careful not to raise the bar so high that you end up swinging from it.

4. Tell Them Where You'll Need the Support

Be clear about when you'll need their close support and when you'll need autonomy, including the autonomy to make mistakes and learn from them. This is not only necessary to protect your leadership; it will help create their ownership for some of your success.

5. Talk Common Concerns

Just like you, your manager has values, maybe the same values, and they struggle with how to understand them and how to live them on the job. Any manager at any level has the same concerns about values fulfillment, human connectivity, and the meaning and legacy of the work they do.

You won't be speaking a foreign language when you talk values and purpose and the real principles of leadership. Discuss your values but inquire after theirs too. Discuss your commitment to living those values over half your waking hours and remember they have these same concerns. This is new common ground that may cause conversations far deeper than those you've had about anything to date.

6. Create Some Context

Take the time to review some things that you'll be doing to drive your leadership *before* you do them, particularly the more unusual ones. Leaping on the conference room table shrieking, "Take my hand," chattering on and on about your values like the house parrot in a methamphetamine lab, arriving at meetings dressed as Marie Antoinette to create a legend around your value of Freedom and dragging one of your people by the ear down fourteen flights of stairs to show that you don't take kindly to any violation of your leadership—these things could use a bit of context. Ahead of time, so your manager doesn't think you've completely lost your mind.

Put your hands on the wheel.

Let the golden age begin.

—BECK

PART 4
GET ON WITH IT

Well all right, well all right.

We'll live and love with

all our might.

—BUDDY HOLLY

PERSONAL IMPLEMENTATION

13

THE TYPICAL MANAGER receives more than a hundred e-mails every day, works more than fifty hours every week and is responsible for more productivity and revenue every year. What you don't need is more to do in order to implement *Bury My Heart at Conference Room B*. You need a fast and simple guide that translates your willingness to embrace the solution into the skill to use it.

This next section provides the first five steps necessary to make it happen. They're in chronological order, since there's really no point in explaining what to do when you make all the mistakes you're going to make until you start making all the mistakes. Never mind that. Let's get started.

STEP ONE: TAKE IT HOME

► HERE, THERE AND EVERYWHERE

There are a lot of advantages to bringing the *Bury My Heart at Conference Room B* process home: You can practice it, refine it, gain extra support for what you're trying to do at work, improve the health of your family and reaffirm the value of living your values. Most importantly, you can help join the divide between who you are and where you are.

Managers have often learned to compartmentalize what have become their twin selves: the one who shows up at work and the one who shows up outside of work. At best this is exhausting—different outfits, different passports—and at worst it's dangerous—different motivations, different standards of fulfillment. Your life need not ever be this way if you aim for the same thing in both worlds.

I've said it before in these pages but as long as I'm the one writing the book I'll keep on yammering about this on your behalf: The key to work/life balance is not escaping work but being who you really are at work. To do that it helps to be who you really are at home.

► FOR YOUR PARTNER

Your partner doesn't work for you—thankfully, or you'd be up on harassment charges of one kind or another. Translating your values to the family unit will require bringing both sets to the table, maybe separate but definitely equal and requiring mutual support to thrive. This will give each of you the benefits of being understood and understanding. It can create a new language for intimacy, possibly the healing of old wounds and the setting of an intentional future.

Individual values—yours and your partner's—can easily be subsumed in the first heat of a relationship, then lost in the slipstream of growing a family. There is often pressure to compromise values at home, sometimes the sign of a relationship that's unstable or has drifted but often something that just happens willingly for the greater good. *There is no greater good* for the both of you or your family than encouraging each other's deepest values.

Stop flailing around with that thing: Put down your anchor at home, in safe harbor. If home is not safe harbor, this process will help it to be.

► HOW TO DO IT

1. Introduce the Process

Explain that you've learned something new about yourself that has made you think about your life and how you want to live it, and that you want to give them the same opportunity. Smile reassuringly because your panicked partner is going to assume what follows is an announcement that you're eloping with the latest attraction at your local zoo.

2. Ask Your Partner to Choose Their Top Three Values

Use the exercises Pick from This List and Confirm Your Choice.

PICK FROM THIS LIST → PP. 70–72

CONFIRM YOUR CHOICE → PP. 78–82

You've already been through this process, so be empathetic to someone wrestling with it for the first time. Don't imply you're already confident about your own values and smugly ask them to guess what they might be. Chances are they'll pick Narcissism, Superiority and Obnoxiousness—not your best platform for the conversation to follow.

3. Share Your Top Values, After They've Shared Theirs

Explain your top values and the Moments of Truth that led to their formation. Ask your partner for their own Moments of Truth. You may think you already know this about each another, but it's possible you don't or that you haven't heard their history connected in this way.

CONNECT THE MOMENTS OF TRUTH → PP. 83–87

• • •

4. Compile a List of Three Values, Drawn from Both of Your Choices

This is a compilation, not a compromise. You don't want to compromise values in the name of your relationship—you want to live them in the name of your relationship. But each of you has already chosen three and if your lists were combined it would become too big to easily prioritize and protect.

Instead, each of you should pick one value from their list of three and then agree on one more. You'll remain aware of the other values and can generally support them, but this combined list will help form your definition of a partnership based on mutual fulfillment.

Explain that only three are used in this process because this gives the ability to master their application, protect and promote them amongst many other priorities and to be clearly known for certain things to those around you. Any longer list risks being a dilution of what's truly most important and the discipline of choosing ensures deep reflection.

Which value should you agree on? Family may be an obvious choice since you are a family and neither of you wants to ditch this choice to the stony glare of their partner. But if Family doesn't make the final cut for either of you, that's okay. It doesn't mean you don't love your family; the strength of a relationship is based on the strength of individual values that are allowed to flourish within it, and that's what this is all about. The same with values of Affection and Integrity—they're part of a healthy relationship and they're implied by engaging in this process.

A good method for selecting the third value is to define what your values give you that makes them so important. Then compare the meanings that each of you chose for your own remaining values. You'll find they're often similar and this will make it easier to pick a value that satisfies you both.

TRANSFERABLE CURRENCY → P. 121

Let's say you and your partner have these values, which are seemingly divergent:

• • •

You	Your Partner
Accomplishment	Affection
Respect	Loyalty
Creativity	Harmony

Now, let's go beyond the literal definition to what each of you might say your values give you that makes them so important:

You	
Accomplishment	Feeling special, trusted by others to deliver
Respect	Being treated fairly and recognized for my contribution
Creativity	Don't have to play the hand that's dealt, options for dealing with the unexpected, challenge, impact on the world
Your Partner	
Affection	Security, feeling special, connected
Loyalty	Protection, being part of something
Harmony	Peace, absence of conflict, looking out for one another, positive energy, little to fear from others

Different values often come from similar personal priorities, giving the ability to satisfy both of you with a single choice:

Accomplishment and Affection Are Compatible	
You	Feeling special, trusted by others to deliver
Your Partner	Feeling special, connected
Respect and Loyalty Are Compatible	
You	Recognized for my contribution
Your Partner	Being part of something

Creativity and Harmony Are Compatible	
You	Options for dealing with the unexpected
Your Partner	Looking out for one another

5. Describe the Bitter Place and Better Place for Your Relationship

Remember, the Bitter Place is any current unsatisfactory state of the values—are they being denied, disrespected or unfulfilled in some way? If so, this doesn't have to be an unpleasant conversation—you're in the midst of coming together to take action on the problem. The Better Place is what life will look like for the two of you when the values are being realized.

DEFINE THE BETTER PLACE → P. 117

BACK THE BETTER WITH THE BITTER → PP. 127–29

6. Agree to Put It into Action as a Partnership Priority

If this means initially formalizing how you do it until it's naturally embedded, so be it. Set a regular time to review how you're using your values to behave with one another and make decisions. Set some rules for living that make it easier for both of you to turn your good intentions into regular behaviors. Keep an eye out for any challenges and celebrate when you do it right. While you're at it, you might want to celebrate deciding not to be complacent about the potential of your relationship.

RULES FOR LIVING → P. 201

▶ FOR YOUR CHILDREN: AGES 8–12

This is a fabulous thing to do with your kids. Young children greet the process of discovery with wonder and delight—better that they play with values than with matches. There are a lot of benefits for you too, including new insights into their self-image and motivations, plus an important reminder of their awareness and determination at such a young age.

▶ HOW TO DO IT

1. Introduce the Importance of Values

Explain that Mom and Dad, or you and your partner, did the same thing to learn more about yourselves and each other and now we're going to share the process as a family. It's always a good, healthy thing for people to understand what's important to one another so we can respect it and protect it—that's what families do.

Mention that sometimes they say you don't understand them or how they're feeling and that this will help. This will also help them understand why you feel so strongly about the things you insist on. It will help us all as a family to understand one another even better.

What are values? They're what help make you the special person that you are. It's what you believe is the most important way to be. It's what makes you happiest when you're living them, saddest or angriest when you're not.

2. Prepare Them for the Process—and Prepare Yourself

Your kids will be predisposed to enjoy this because it's all about them and there's interest and respect implied. Still, it needs to be an engaging experience: serious enough to reinforce the importance but fun in the exploration and decision. Start by explaining that this isn't a test. Whatever is right for them is the right answer.

They may have a natural inclination to choose certain values because they think they're supposed to. If they leap immediately on values you suspect are picked to please you, make sure they have an understanding of each one on the list before deciding. This is your guarantee that it's going to be important learning for you both.

This process isn't about imprinting moral lessons—that's a separate parenting issue. It's about understanding your child's individual values preferences—how they see the world, all on their own—and so they shouldn't have to pick what you want them to. They're going to try to please you, though, and will be checking you closely for signals. If you have to scratch your nose while they're breezily skipping over Integrity on the list, Let. It. Itch.

3. Allow Them to Choose Their Own Values

Use the same 10-5-3 reduction process that you applied. The list of values below has been abbreviated and revised for younger children.

PICK FROM THIS LIST → PP. 69–72

My Value	It Means
1. Acceptance	People like you for who you are. Others want to include you.
2. Accomplishment	Setting goals and meeting them
3. Affection	Love, deep friendship
4. Altruism	Giving to those who have less than you
5. Competence	Liking to be really good at something and wanting to constantly get better at it
6. Creativity	Imagination. New ways of seeing and doing things.
7. Fairness	People are treated the way they deserve to be treated
8. Family	Looking out for one another, supporting each other, doing things together
9. Freedom	The ability to make your own choices
10. Individuality	Being your own person
11. Integrity	Doing what you say and saying what you mean
12. Intelligence	Being smart about something. Being seen as smart.
13. Learning	Discovering new things. New ways of seeing the world.
14. Loyalty	Supporting the people you care about, sometimes even if other people don't
15. Order	Things make sense and are as they should be. Your boundaries are respected.

My Value	It Means
16. Power	Ability to influence people and situations around you
17. Recognition	Being noticed for who you are and what you do
18. Respect	Who you are is important to other people
19. Security	Feeling safe in relationships with family and friends
20. Spirituality	Kindness, respect for all living things, doing the right thing

4. Discuss Their Choices but Don't Debate Them

With very young children you should discuss each of the values to confirm their understanding. This is a great teaching experience although it does have a potential downside: Your explanation may have to include acting the words out. Great if you have Creativity as a value; not so great if you have Respect.

Help your children confirm their choices by asking for examples of how a particular value is important to them at school, with their friends and in their relationship with you. Ask for specific situations, which will be easier for them to talk about than general concepts. Discuss how this affects them—their happiness and how they use their values to make good choices.

They're going to want to know your values. Explain these and provide them with an explanation of why you chose them—they may well have formed at the same age as your children's. Pick a few situations common to you both—where decisions have to be made, where there is stress or temptation to compromise—and discuss how each of you would handle them based on your individual values.

Let them take all the time they need to decide and change their mind as they need to. At this young age, your children may not make lasting choices, but involvement in the process is as important as the outcome.

Be on the alert for any signs that your child is revealing signs of helplessness, isolation or anger in which values they choose as important—such as Security, Power and Respect. Sometimes it can be a sign that they're not able to live their own values or have concluded their own priorities are considered unimportant. It might be a sign of what they want most from you.

5. Explain How Their Values Will Be Treated within the Family

It's important that kids grow up with a sense of what is theirs and believing that their parents respect it. Kids being kids, of course, they're going to want to know the implications of this respect. Specifically, how far can they can stretch it?

You're still the Big Dog and you don't give up any parental authority by encouraging their values. You're not licensing them freedom to do whatever they want, even if your little puppy chose Freedom on that assumption. It's not the literal definition of the word that is the value; it's the translation of that value into meaning and living. You can therefore inform them that with all due respect to their value of Creativity, when they earn like the Jonas Brothers they can live like one of the Jonas Brothers. In the meantime, they'd better clean their room or they'll be living like one of the Brothers Karamazov—particularly the one called Ivan, who descended into raving madness after the devil visited him and mocked his beliefs.

It's a reasonable proposition for your children that they'll secure protection of their values by first protecting the family values, which have been decided by their parents. It's just another version of "This is *my* house!" which they've heard a few times before.

They should have to earn protection of their values in another way, by demonstrating that their choices are important enough to them to be worth your support. This means they can't regularly violate their values at school or allow them to be easily dismissed by circumstances or the sway of their friends.

This is a tall order for small folk, and you'll have to help them help themselves. Translate their values into rules for living at home and check in regularly to ensure they aren't experiencing conflict or dismissal anywhere in their lives about what's most important to them. As a family, you'll need to talk about values constantly and reinforce when they're supported or violated. Most important is that you'll have to clearly demonstrate an allegiance to your own values: That's where they'll take the hint that this is the right thing to do.

▶ FOR YOUR OLDER CHILDREN: AGES 13–18

As parents, we judge ourselves by our intentions, which are typically pure and logical. We judge our teenagers by their actions, which are often suspect and delusional.

Checking the wrong instruction manual is what causes a lot of these actions. Children at this age are prone to look outside to define what's inside. If their sense of self comes from external sources—peer pressure, pop culture and personal electronics—it's unstable. This process will help them define how to act, armed with a greater awareness of who they are. They'll be less hungry for self-definition and less susceptible to unhealthy or harebrained influences.

▶ HOW TO DO IT

1. Introduce the Importance of Values

Explain that Mom and Dad, or you and your partner, did the same thing to learn more about yourselves and each other and now you're going to share the process with them. It's always a good, healthy thing for people to understand what's important to each other so we can respect it and protect it—that's what families do to be good to one another.

Mention that sometimes they say you don't understand them or how they're feeling and that this will help. This will also help them understand why you feel so strongly about the things you insist on. It will help you all as a family to understand one another even better. Make clear that they have a lot of choices to make about who they are and how they want to act in certain situations. Understanding their values will allow them to know what the right choice is, according to their own definition.

What are values? They're what help make you the special person that you are. They're what you believe is the most important way to be. They're what make you happiest when you're living them, saddest or angriest when you're not.

2. Prepare Them for the Process—and Prepare Yourself

Start by explaining that this isn't a test. Whatever is right for them is the right answer.

Your children may have a natural inclination to choose certain values because they think they're supposed to—or if they're sixteen, often because they think they're not supposed to. Make sure they spend some time considering all of the possible choices.

As with your younger children, this process isn't about embedding moral lessons—that remains a separate parenting issue. It's about respecting individual values preferences—how they see the world all on their own—and so they shouldn't have to pick what you want them to. Find a sturdy stick you can bite on when they skip past Cooperation and Learning only to leap on Respect. Remind yourself that *life* is a process too, as you gnaw through the wood.

3. Allow Them to Choose Their Own Values

Use a version of the same 10-5-3 reduction process that you applied. The list of values below has been abbreviated and revised for teenagers.

PICK FROM THIS LIST → PP. 69-72

My Value	It Means
1. Acceptance	People like you for who you are. Others want to include you.
2. Accomplishment	Succeeding in reaching goals
3. Adventure	Taking risks, new experiences
4. Affection	Love, deep friendship
5. Altruism	Giving to those who have less than you
6. Commitment	Dedication to cause, satisfaction in obligation
7. Competence	Doing things well, consistent self-improvement
8. Competitiveness	Besting performance in yourself or others
9. Cooperation	Pulling together toward a common goal

My Value	It Means
10. Creativity	Imagination, new ways of doing and seeing
11. Enlightenment	Pursuit of awareness that feeds the soul
12. Fairness	Equal consideration, rights and opportunities
13. Family	Community that looks out for one another, supporting each other, doing things together
14. Freedom	Independence, free will
15. Fun	Enjoyment and perspective
16. Health	Well-being of mind, body and spirit
17. Individuality	Originality, self-expression
18. Integrity	Doing what you say, saying what you mean
19. Intelligence	Acquiring and applying knowledge
20. Loyalty	Remaining faithful to a person or cause
21. Order	Respect for procedure and organization, calm
22. Passion	Enthusiasm, powerful attraction to do something
23. Peace	Calm, centered, free from stress
24. Power	Ability to influence people and conditions
25. Recognition	Attention, positive notice
26. Respect	Treating others well, being treated well
27. Security	Feeling safe in relationships with family and friends, or financially

My Value	It Means
28. Service	To be of assistance and support
29. Spirituality	Moral compass, belief in higher purpose, respect for all living things
30. Teaching	Passing knowledge on to others

4. Discuss Their Choices but Don't Debate Them

Teenagers should be old enough to understand the greater meaning of their values, so move their thinking beyond the literal definition to what makes their choices so important to them—the more clarification they have the more they'll protect the values. If they need help to start considering, ask for examples of how a particular value is important to them at school, with their friends, at work, in the things they most like to do and in their relationship with you. Discuss how each value affects their happiness and how they use it to make good choices.

Let them take all the time they need to decide and change their mind as they need to. Involvement in the process is as important as the outcome.

Be on the alert for any signs that your teenager is revealing signs of helplessness, isolation or anger in which values they choose as important—such as Security, Power and Respect. Sometimes it can be a sign that they're not able to live their own values or have concluded their own priorities are considered unimportant. Relationships, responsibilities and considerations of the future are changing for them as they get older; it can be an unsettling time.

5. Engage Them in Discussion about Their Values in Action

The Bitter Place is still any current unsatisfactory state of their top values while the Better Place is what life will look like for them when those values are regularly realized. Ask them to define both places in the major arenas of their life—at home, at school, with friends and in regard to major decisions.

DEFINE THE BETTER PLACE → P. 117

BACK THE BETTER WITH THE BITTER → PP. 127–29

Revisit some decisions they've made and ask them to preview some that are coming up. How did their values hold up in the past and what pressure may there be to compromise them in the future? Do they know peers who've compromised their values? Do they admire anyone who holds strongly to their own values?

Discuss how their values affect them—their happiness and how they use them to make good choices. Pick a few situations—where decisions have to be made, where there is stress or temptation to compromise—common to you both and discuss how each of you would handle them based on your individual values.

6. Explain How Their Values Will Be Treated within the Family

Teenagers are at a vulnerable age, equally susceptible to uncertainty and influence. While you may have every confidence in them to make good choices, now is the time when the family should remain extra supportive of their values as the driver for those choices. This is also when your children should be extra aware of the consequences for acting in support of their values, or failing to. It's a great perspective for them to build now, before they're at an age to make decisions that their allowance won't cover.

One way to help them build it is by insisting they support the family's values first as a way of ensuring your support for their own. Others include helping them translate values into rules for living and checking in regularly to ensure they aren't experiencing conflict about what's most important to them or how to apply it. As a family, you'll need to talk about values constantly and reinforce when they're supported or violated.

RULES FOR LIVING → P. 201

Explain that the people they interact with may have different values. It's important not to judge them for this. Many people may be unaware of their values, including many adults who will go through life without understanding what means the most to them and so live a life of less fulfillment and more compromise, where the choices they make aren't connected to the way they really want to live. Tell them you want a better life for them. Concerned that you're no longer a primary role model to a headstrong teenager? This will go a long way to remedy that situation.

▶ FOR YOUR FAMILY

As soon as you've agreed on values with your partner and helped your children to their own discovery, it's time to translate it all to life in the family.

▶ HOW TO DO IT

1. Remember That There Can Be a Difference between Values and Morals

Don't worry if the individual values you and your partner have compiled didn't include Integrity, Family, Spirituality and other moral foundations. You are not abdicating these as important in the family and can insist on them same as always. But you are also insisting to your children that it's important to understand one's own values, whatever they may be, and practice them in life.

2. Reveal Your Own Values and Moments of Truth

Clarification of your core values is going to be a transcendent moment for your kids: heavenly insight into what makes you tick; new ability to relate to you as a human being, not just a parental unit; and an obvious key to predicting your behavior, especially as it relates to their own behavior.

Offering Moments of Truth is going to be the signal to your children that this whole thing is for real since they usually only get an explanation of The Why tagged to The What when something important is afoot. As much as you can, give them an understanding of how your values formed early on, when you were close to their age. This will be more relevant for them—and a lot smarter for you than trying to edit a description of your own adult Year of Bad Choices.

3. Describe the Bitter and Better Places for the Whole Family

What would it look like for everyone in the family if these values were not taken seriously? People couldn't trust as easily, behavior wouldn't be predictable, it would be harder to understand decisions or get dependable signals about the reasons for rewards or punishments. But just the opposite is true if there is constant respect for and protection of values chosen by the family and family members.

4. Explain That You Need Their Help to Make It Happen

Time to play the Maslow Hierarchy of Needs: Home Version. Provide your children the opportunity to realize significance, belonging and self-worth in their role of supporting the family's values and they'll be more interested in doing it.

GIVE THEM SOMETHING FOR THE TRIP → P. 133

Something as important as sustaining how the family is going to treat one another is going to require contribution by the entire family. Everyone has the choice to protect the values or violate them, and everyone wins and suffers accordingly. The family is going to have to be smart, resilient and loving—trusting and trustworthy.

5. Enforce and Reinforce

All the rules for shaping behavior apply here: Talk about values constantly. Reinforce not just what was done by anyone in the family but how it was done and celebrate if it was in accordance with the values. Take lapses seriously but use them as a method for constant improvement.

Bring your children into more family decisions so they can learn how values become a primary tool for making the right choice. Remember that someday they're going to be doing the same with their own family and, if the fates conspire to provide them with a management career, for their own teams. When those days come, you want them explaining that it was their parents who taught them the importance of sticking to their values. Not their therapist.

▶ FOR YOUR FRIENDS

Whether you'd extend the definition of family to include some cherished friends or whether that *is* your definition of family—a chosen community rather than an inherited one—this process still works and is still important for you.

▶ HOW TO DO IT

Think you know your friends? Think they know themselves? Try this: Gather them together for some beer and values (this is thirsty work) and let them take the values confirmation exercises.

1. Have Them Choose Their Own Values

Give them the same eighteen minutes to do this as you had (10, then 5, then 3). The purpose is to point out that it's tougher than they might have thought. You might want to write down your own guess as to what the values are for each of them. Be sure to have them move past the literal definitions to what these values really give them in their lives.

PICK FROM THIS LIST → PP. 70–72

DEFINE THE BETTER PLACE → P. 117

2. Confirm Their Choice

Staying with the tougher-than-they-may-have-thought theme, have them take this diagnostic to confirm their values selections.

CONFIRM YOUR CHOICE → PP. 78–82

3. Connect the Moments of Truth

Start by sharing your own values—you might ask them to guess first. Then share your story about how you know this to be true. Then ask them to share their own Moment of Truth stories.

CONNECT THE MOMENTS OF TRUTH → PP. 83–87

4. Explore Some Big Questions

You won't have time for them all but put a few on the table for them to pounce on as a group. If they have an ounce of pounce left in them by that time.

TALK TO YOURSELF, TALK TO OTHERS → P. 88

5. Explain the Bitter Place and Better Place Concepts

These will be thought-provoking concepts for your friends to consider. If not, you might consider getting some new friends.

DEFINE THE BETTER PLACE → P. 117

BACK THE BETTER WITH THE BITTER → PP. 127–29

● ● ●

Personally, I have an absolute criterion for choosing friends: They must be weight-bearing. I don't go through each day assuming some nutso pressure is going to drop on me or my family, but if it does I want to know my friends are the kind of people who will step up strongly to help. It's the same standard I hold myself to on their behalf.

If this is important to you, an awareness of your friends' values will create new understanding and deeper bonds, key ingredients in achieving trust at this level.

▶ FOR YOURSELF

If you're currently a family unit of one, or if the only human interaction you require is a stick of gum and a mirror, bringing the *Bury My Heart at Conference Room B* process home will still help you make decisions consistent with your values and set your own rules for living.

▶ HOW TO DO IT

Hopefully the values identification and confirmation exercises in the book already have you thinking about application to your entire life, not just life at work. Return to them now with life outside of work in mind:

1. Confirm What Each Value Gives You in Your Life

You will already have done this as part of the original exercise, but go back to it now thinking about life outside of work and confirm: What makes them so important to you?

TRANSFERABLE CURRENCY → P. 121

2. Describe the Bitter and Better Places for Your Personal Circumstances

This was also part of the original version you did, but you have time to do it again—it's not like anyone's on you about cleaning out the garage.

DEFINE THE BETTER PLACE → P. 117

BACK THE BETTER WITH THE BITTER → PP. 127–29

◉ ◉ ◉

Any sappy refrigerator magnet sold at the car wash will tell you this: You've got to be your own best friend. This process is a great way to do it. In the future, should you choose to make eye contact with some target significant other, it will have given you the attractive confidence that belongs to the self-aware.

STEP TWO: DECLARE IT

This time the struggle is for our freedom,
this time the struggle is for our independence.
—SHEIKH MUJIBUR RAHMAN, MARCH 7, 1971

Let those who have been wearing themselves out
in both body and soul now work for a double honor.
—POPE URBAN II, NOVEMBER 27, 1095

We are talking about a society in which there will be no roles
other than those chosen, or those earned.
—GLORIA STEINEM, JULY 10, 1971

I am your king. You are French. There is the enemy. Charge!
—HENRY IV, MARCH 14, 1590

Every great movement of a people has been ignited by a galvanizing speech. If you want your people to seriously commit to making your own Better Place happen, you're not only going to have to announce what you stand for, you're going to have to do it in an entirely new way. Here are the four steps needed to construct your all-important first declaration. And the one step that matters most.

1. "These Are My Deepest Personal Values"

Example:
"I believe in many things, but these values are most important to me: Family, which gives me unconditional support, open and honest communication, and contribution to the lives of others. Integrity, which means I can trust the information given to me, there is respect for the truth as I see it, and that I have the ability to learn from my attempts and grow from my mistakes. Spirituality, which gives me a moral compass, inner peace and respect for all living things.

"This is what I've learned about living. I refuse to do without the benefits of these values at work, a place I spend over half my waking hours, and I refuse to have people I care about do without them either."

2. "This Is How We Are Living Now"

Example:
"We are not getting the benefits of these values today. We don't always support one another. Everybody's under pressure and instead

of looking out for one another we're looking for ways to gain an edge on each other. We don't talk, we don't listen—we don't really communicate at all.

"We accept all the pressures on us to deviate from what we know to be the best way to serve the company and then we consider ourselves victims of forces beyond our control. This isn't a safe place to learn or grow because it's not a safe place to make a mistake.

"There is constant anxiety in the team because we haven't taken a stand on the right way to do business and we let the agendas and priorities of others decide that for us. We're not even sure what we stand for as the people who make up this team."

3. "This Is How We Are Going to Live"

Example:

"This will be a place where you will be able to make decisions safely because you'll be able to depend on information coming to you as being the truth, the whole truth and the truth on time. We will respect the truth as you see it even if it's not the popular truth. This will be a place where it is going to be all right to be accountable. You can try things if you believe in them, you can admit if it didn't work out as planned and you can learn from it. You will have the chance to grow every minute of every day.

"This will be a place of open, honest communication. Under pressure, this team will never turn on this team. Instead, this team will come together to protect this team.

"This will be a place where we do business the right way—ethically, with respect for everyone we deal with inside and outside of this organization. We will never lose that sense of what's right despite any pressure or temptation to compromise. We're not only going to execute the work that comes our way, we're also going to leverage the fine minds and fierce hearts here for a greater purpose than just the day-to-day effort.

"How are we going to make these things work together in this company, with all that we have to do? I don't know that but I do know this: It's exactly what we're going to do."

. . .

4. "It's Important and It's Going to Take a Team of Special People to Make It Happen"

Example:

"I can't do this by myself. It's going to take a team and not just any team. It's going to take this team.

"We can't provide for our family outside the job unless we behave like a family right here. When we do, we'll have open, honest communication and unconditional support, and we'll be able to depend on one another if things get tough.

"The respect we show to all people inside and outside of this organization is going to determine the respect they show to us. At the end of the day, the question is, how did we maintain our personal integrity amidst the pressures that surrounded us? We're here for a reason and that reason can be as meaningful as we want to make it.

"It's not going to be easy. We'll have to be the kind of people who watch one another's backs. We're going to have to be tough and focused so that nobody can break apart our commitment to mutual success. We're going to have to be smart enough to figure out how we want to work and strong enough not to be stopped from making it happen. Things can get crazy around here. Fine—we're going to be crazier than that in our dedication to what we know is right: We'll be brave and impossible to stop."

● ● ●

WRAP IT UP. I'LL TAKE IT.

By this point you're probably used to representing your company. Representing yourself is a whole different matter. Your initial statement about who you are and why has to reset the standard of what's possible in the relationship between you and your people.

Explaining your values, the Bitter Place and the Better Place, and what's in it for your people along the way are all important, but they're not enough. This first declaration from you has to grab their attention like you've never done before. The best method for doing it is to also reveal Moments of Truth—the stories of how you know the values are real to you. Where they came from and how you learned them. The intimate and profound personal experiences, be they glorious or traumatic, that shaped your acute self-awareness.

Living out loud may not be your thing. You may consider it unnecessary, inappropriate or even dangerous to disclose such information at work. You may prefer a moat filled with snarly sea creatures guarding the breach between your life and your people's involvement in it. But consider what's at stake here: Your ability to meet your deepest personal values depends on your ability to garner their support. If they perceive this as just another management message, you're not going to get it.

Like most managers, there's a good chance you have used and abused your credibility over the years with constant dramatic *life-as-we-know-it-will-come-to-an-end-unless* type of announcements. As much as you're used to delivering those management messages, your people are used to hearing them, often with limited attention or belief. How are your people supposed to recognize that they're hearing something different and more important?

This time, for this kind of impact, you're going to have to go deeper, appear vulnerable and step out from behind whatever protection your job title affords you. You are saying to your people, "This is what I've learned is most important about living. I'm not willing to do without the benefits of that learning for over half my waking hours and I'm not willing to let people I'm close to do without it either." By disclosing how your unshakable view of life priorities was formed, you are offering proof of your values commitment.

THE LESSONS OF FLORENCE TAYLOR
true tales from the *bury my heart* files

It is a savage yet triumphant personal history, never revealed to most of her friends and certainly never to anyone who works for her. Florence Taylor has decided to tell her story.

Florence is a director in her company, and her company is well known. She was reluctant to have it featured in the book and agreed only if I wouldn't use her real name, the name of her company, or the town where this incident occurred. In this one case, I agreed. It was the least I could do; Florence herself still bears the scars of her values awareness, both emotional and physical.

■　■　■

"I grew up in a very small town in the Deep South. There were two schools in our town: the white school and the black school. Since I'm black I went to the black school, which didn't have as many teachers or books or fun things as the white school. But I was a smart little girl and my mother made up for the lack of resources when I got home every day. Before I could go out and play we would sit at the dining room table and she would take down a big old encyclopedia from the shelf and teach me about the world.

"One day I brought home a report card that was so good my mother said, 'I think we can get you into the white school. Do you want to go?' 'Yes!' I said, because I was a smart girl and I wanted to learn. I didn't know that the school district was under a lot of federal pressure to integrate. Our family talked about it and decided that if the school would accept me I would go—as long as my two older brothers transferred with me. My brothers didn't want to go but they loved their little sister and so they agreed. We would be the first black children at the school.

"I had only two dresses and I got to wear my church dress on my first day in school! I was assigned a seat in the back next to a little redheaded white girl and I immediately became best friends with her, the way little girls do. When the bell rang for recess I went out to the schoolyard to play with my new friend and her other friends. All of the girls were in the schoolyard and all of the boys were playing on the football field. A large wire fence separated the two areas. My new friend told me that boys and girls used to play together, but since my two brothers were here now the school had put up the fence to separate the boys from the girls.

"We were playing and screaming and laughing when we heard screaming of a different kind from the edge of the schoolyard. I looked up to see four huge men on horseback with masks on, carrying baseball bats. They were riding right at us. Everyone ran toward the school building. The teachers got there first and locked the doors behind them. As I was running I could hear my brothers yelling my name. They were clawing at the fence, trying to save me, but the fence was too high.

"I was a fast little girl, weighed almost nothing and most of it was legs. I was already almost to the bleacher seats stacked against the wall of the school building. I knew if I could scramble under those bleachers the horses couldn't get to me. I was just about to roll under the seats when I heard a scream I thought I recognized. I turned around and saw that one of the riders had grabbed my new friend by the hair—she had been playing with me—and was holding her a couple of feet off the ground. She was screaming and sobbing.

"I didn't even stop to think. I just turned around and ran at that man on the horse. He was holding my friend on the left side of the horse. This horse was so big and it was sweating and its eyes were wild and glaring at me. It was trying to move around to hit me with its foot. I ran to the man's right side and sunk my teeth into his leg, biting him as hard as I could.

"The good news is that he dropped my friend, but he picked me up instead. He dragged me by my arm across the concrete and two blocks outside the schoolyard. My Sunday dress got torn off. I was bruised all over, the skin on my back and side and left leg was in ribbons and they tell me that I lost a lot of blood. He left me lying in the street but I don't really remember that.

"My mother came to the hospital every day for five weeks. Every day she brought my school lessons and that old encyclopedia and she would help me study the best I could. When I got out, she asked me what I wanted to do. 'I want to go back to the white school and graduate,' I said. And I did."

■   ■   ■

"I am a grown woman now. I am a successful executive. I am a wife and I am a mother. In this life I have had an opportunity to learn what is most important to me. What is most important to me is loyalty. The little white girl from that school is still my best friend today. I'm not willing to live without loyalty in my life and I'm not willing to have people I care about live without it.

"We have a lot of pressures on our team these days. You're working very hard and we often don't get the cooperation we need from other departments. Things aren't always easy for us and I know that. I know this will change because we will be the ones to change it—I just can't tell you when it will change.

"But I can tell you this: If you are working for me, and you ever get into trouble trying to do the right thing . . .

"I'm coming back for you."

THE POWER SOURCE

Will revealing yourself in this way cause a loss of power, affect your ability to manage, be used against you in some way? I've recommended this process for many managers for many years and never—not once, not close—have I ever known it to be rated as foolish by employees, perceived differently than intended or subsequently used to manipulate their manager. I've received a lot of reports of other kinds of reactions, though. Reactions like these:

"I have suffered from a serious, chronic illness for many years. How it has limited me and how I have learned to overcome my limitations and struggle on has formed a lot of who I am. I have never told any of my employees about being sick. I felt it was not their business and not their concern and it would only weaken my position as their manager. Considering your process, I decided to gather my entire team in a room and explain my values and where they come from. At the end of my talk I thanked my family, which has helped me through the darkest times. Someone in the room shouted, 'We're your family too and we'll take care of you!' Everyone stood and applauded. I was in that room. I watched this happen. What I thought about the potential of people to come together in the workplace has changed forever."

● ● ●

"I have now delivered my leadership declaration to my team of thirty-five folks. That was the hardest thing that I've ever done in my life. I was delivering it to people I have to face every day. Were they going to respect me after we shared twenty very emotional minutes? I didn't know who was going to throw up first, them or me.

"No one threw up. When I finished my speech, the room was silent. Absolutely. No one spoke. No one moved. I was patiently waiting to have a heart attack. A few folks finally made a few comments. I had to leave the room first to get everyone else to leave. When I returned to the conference room, one lone team member was still sitting at the table. His comment: 'Wow! That's the most powerful message I've ever heard. I've been at this company for fifteen years, and I've NEVER heard anything that motivational.'

"As you predicted, folks sent me e-mails and stopped by my office. All the comments were positive and ranged from the simple 'Thank you' to 'You described the kind of place that I want to work. I don't think we are there, but just knowing that you feel this way gives me confidence that we can get there.'

"For the first time ever, I heard directly from my team exactly how important and meaningful my leadership is to them. They are starved for emotional connection. It is a lesson I will never forget."

◉　◉　◉

"I had to translate my values into the workplace in order for my team to become real to me and for me to become real to my team. The level of commitment that I've gotten from my team since I announced them is incredible. When I hear, 'After you told us who you are, this has been the best year ever for us' and 'We don't ever want you to leave,' these are sure signs that it was worth it."

◉　◉　◉

"*Bury My Heart at Conference Room B* stripped me down to my essence yet gave me the confidence to share my deepest values and where they come from. Still, I felt naked in front of a room full of people, without any PowerPoint or product announcements. The crazy thing is I came out the other side with strength and resolve and support from people that I lacked just twenty-four hours before."

◉　◉　◉

"I did this talk with my people and the response was absolutely amazing! There's no way to understand the impact until you do it. You could feel deep emotion sweep that room."

◉　◉　◉

"The experience of delivering this presentation blew me away. Apparently, I brought a lot of tears to the eyes of the people there. It clearly put me in a different light and, in some odd way, gave me more credibility in the company."

◉　◉　◉

"Giving my values speech was so hard! In fact, I don't think I have ever worked so hard to deliver what ended up being a seventeen-minute talk. I mean, I literally spent hours and hours on it and I enlisted a number of friends in the process. But I did it and gave the talk last week to the organization—about 120 folks or so. The group really responded. I got great verbal feedback over the next weeks, and I am really pleased that I went forward with this. The amount of effort, energy and angst that I've put into this process was totally worthwhile. People know me a lot better now, they know what we stand for and, most importantly, they know why."

◉　◉　◉

"I got up on stage in front of 250 people and told one of the most personal stories of my life. And people said they would follow me. Then I talked to my six direct reports and the reaction was even stronger. My team has taken on a new light of creativity and collaboration that I would not have imagined. And the business partners they work with are referencing my top value as characteristic of my team."

◉　◉　◉

"After my talk people made comments like: 'It's really wonderful that you have shared with us what your drivers are; it really makes a difference to know what are the most important things for you'; 'This is the first time I've known this about anyone who has ever been my manager. Thank you, thank you, thank you'; 'This makes it safer for us to be vulnerable, too, and be more open and more ourselves.'"

● ● ●

"A week or so after my talk I started getting e-mails about it. The one that hit me the hardest was from someone who said, 'We always knew you were a good manager. We just didn't know you were human.'"

● ● ●

THE FULL MEANING OF THE BLANK STARE

Get ready for this: You may pour your heart out to your people and they may sit and stare at you without saying anything. This is called "listening"—they're *listening* to you. You might not be used to this as a manager.

The first conversation isn't going to happen with you anyway. Delivered correctly, your message will cause the employee culture to drag impressions back to its own cave to ponder what just happened. Why did you divulge this private, personal information? You didn't have to. You could have simply insisted that this is the way things are going to be and they would have expected to trudge dutifully behind you down a road you'd named after yourself. The only rational explanation the culture can arrive at is that you must have wanted them to understand that what you just told them is more important than anything you've ever told them before.

One speech won't convince your people of anything, but that's not the battle you have to win. Your people have to leave your talk believing that *you* deeply believe what you just told them. This is rare enough to set context for your actions that come next. You've opened a file with the employee culture; anything you do to show you mean what you said will become a proof point of your intentions and a clue to predicting your actions. Understanding what's most important to you allows the culture to put itself in safe orbit around you—it now knows what will make you happiest (supporting your values) or unhappiest (not supporting your values).

The strongest thing you can do is to make yourself willingly vulnerable. Most impressive to others is when you do it on their behalf: It's not an easy offering for them to reject. Whatever you think it might cost you is nothing compared to what it will have earned you. You will have gained support for your message that you cannot have gotten any other way.

For years, managers have been sending me the e-mails that people sent them after their presentation. E-mails like these:

"My words won't capture the spirit you created in yesterday's presentation. You stood and delivered an exceptional message. After you left, folks were so incredibly excited to be part of this team and truly resonated with your message. You created over fifty agents of change yesterday, and we have to continue to feed this if we want it to make a difference. So I'm clear, this is not about business issues or tactics, this is about the values component of your message."

◉ ◉ ◉

"My regard for you has doubled after I heard about the values that are important for you. I will try my best to follow in your footsteps."

◉ ◉ ◉

"I was riveted by each and every syllable you said. I want to thank you for your efforts and I am committed to your ongoing success. Please reach out to me if there is anything I can do to assist you."

◉ ◉ ◉

"Kudos to you for having the courage to speak about yourself, challenge us on some of the tougher and more unspoken issues, and for opening yourself up to your trusted team. You set a great example in your organization today."

◉ ◉ ◉

"I was completely blown away by your commitment and bravery."

◉ ◉ ◉

"The buzz in the room after you left, and I spoke to many people since I was the last to leave, was incredible. I know your talk took guts to give and I am so glad I was there to witness it. Sometimes the things that have the greatest impact are those that are the toughest to do. I gained a whole new level of trust for you yesterday and I would say that I know you and have more access to you than most at the company. If your talk can have that kind of impact on me, it had significantly more on the others."

● ● ●

► HOW TO DO IT

1. Be Sure You're Ready

Check out history's most successful leaders: They weren't faking it. Neither were the people who chose to follow them. Your employee culture is going to expect you to mean what you say, so before you say it make sure that you do. Even if you've never officially announced them, are you at least somewhat true to your values?

If not, you can't blame your team for being skeptical. If you regularly insist on Productivity with no mention of any greater meaning then summon them together to announce that you've been to the mountaintop and decided what is most important to you is Spirituality, they're going to be thinking, "You're telling us we have to work on Christmas Day—just get to the point."

You have one first chance to make a plausible first impression here. Depending on how you've shown up in the past, your plausibility may have to include an admission that you haven't been taking your values seriously or hadn't been considering how to dramatically improve the quality of your team's working conditions. This accountability won't hurt you. It will be perceived as the kind of honest self-discovery that precedes real dedication to a cause.

2. Start It

Call your people together to announce the platform for your leadership:

- Your top three values
- Moments of Truth
- Bitter Place
- Better Place
- What's in it for them along the way (significance, belonging and self-worth)

You don't need a Moment of Truth for every value—give them one or two and you'll be granted credibility that the rest of your values are just as real to you. Your Moment of Truth story can be about good things or bad things, about big things or small things. What counts is that it is a detailed description of how you know that the value is real to you—where it came from, when it was tested, when you ignored it to your peril or learned to respect it, how it has influenced you.

3. Show It

Your people have to see that it costs you something, that you have chosen to divulge information you didn't have to in order to convince them of the intensity of your conviction. Your people don't want slick; they want real. You won't lose an ounce of credibility if you get emotional or stumble over some words. They're not judging you as a professional speaker here and they're not paying to see you. They're being paid to see you. Cling to this.

4. Limit It

Keep your talk to 20–30 minutes. Any longer and you'll find yourself answering questions about how and when the Better Place is going to be achieved. That's not the purpose of this talk—it's a declaration of intention, not a tactical overview. Not to mention that you don't have a clue as to how it's going to happen—that's why you need them.

5. Focus It

It's often a hassle and an expense to bring your team together. Yet try not to use the meeting to discuss *anything* else. This will certainly be noted by your people: Evidently there is nothing more important than what you have to tell them. If you have to combine topics, do this first and put a long break before the start of the regular agenda.

6. Consolidate It

If you have a big organization try to get as many as possible for your first presentation since by the time you get to a second meeting all the people present at the first one will have delivered it for you. If you can't bring everybody together, use videoconferencing but try to avoid a phone call and never use e-mail to communicate such an important, personal message. If only a few can't attend, send those people an individually signed hard copy of what you're going to say on that call with instructions not to open it until the call starts.

7. Don't Even Try It

I can't tell you how many times I've been asked by anxious managers, "Does my Moment of Truth have to be real?"

STEP THREE: PROVE IT

When you declare your values and vision of a Better Place, you're announcing to the employee culture what you stand for (*Good, good*). You're explaining to the culture exactly where to look to decide if you can be trusted (*What?*). You're betting your entire personal credibility on the ability to protect your values and vision against every stress, temptation, performance pressure and contrary management decision that unexpectedly descends on you from above (*Hey, wait a minute!*).

There are only two things you can do about it: Earn trust and screw up.

EARN TRUST

You may think your people already trust you, but that's manager trust. You're not asking them for that much as a manager: Show up, do your job, leave me alone, go home. Ask for their help to take the team to a Better Place based on your newly revealed personal values and you may find out how reluctant they are to give you leadership trust. You're going to have to earn that kind of trust like leaders do, through consistency and passion, and by how you make mistakes and cause others to.

▶ CONSISTENCY AND THE NOT-SO-SMALL THING

Presumably, you consider yourself to be an honest, hardworking manager who has every reason to be trusted by your people.

As an honest and hardworking manager who has every reason to be trusted by your people, how many times have you told an employee that you'll meet them "Tuesday at 10:30" only to get a call from your own manager or a crazed customer or both Tuesday at 10:20, and have to blow off that meeting without thinking about it? How many times have you told an employee, "I'll get back to you with my answer on that by the end of the day," and by the time you realize it's the end of the day, it's the end of the decade? How many times have you promised an employee that you'll meet on Monday to review their performance only to have Monday become someday?

Do your people know that you don't have total control over your schedule? Yes. Do they know that you're basically a decent person trying to do a tough job? Yes. Have they figured out how to work around these constant, small violations of trust from you? Yes.

Will these constant small violations of trust hurt you as a manager? No. Will these constant small violations of trust hurt you as a leader? No. They'll kill you as a leader.

When you're asking for trust as a leader you're asking for a lot. Trusting you as a leader is risky business—your people have to commit themselves intellectually, emotionally, spiritually, physically and financially. Before your people commit to following you, they're going to look hard for the Big Thing—are you committed deep in your heart to taking them to this Better Place? This presents a problem for them: How can they see deep inside you? They can only see the small things, what's outside.

Warning: The small things have just become the Big Thing.

In the absence of any other way to judge what they can't see, your people will decide to have faith in you based on what they *can* see. Those small violations of trust that your people have learned to accommodate from you as a manager will now take on a far greater importance. If you don't realize this has shifted on you as you shift from manager to leader, you're not going to be able to establish a critical component of trust.

Is this fair? So you didn't get back to them about some small thing as promised. Your people should understand and get over it. Oh, they'll understand and get over it. They just won't have faith in your leadership.

► HOW TO DO IT

1. Stop It

Stop making commitments you know in advance you have no chance of keeping: Just shut up. Don't say, "I'll meet you Tuesday at 10:30," when you know you can't possibly guarantee such a thing in your ever-changing schedule. (I always tell people in my company, "I've got summer and winter open—which one works best for you?") Don't make any commitment, even casually, just to keep things moving or buy yourself some time.

2. Apologize for It

Make amends for any small violations of trust. Your people will appear to shrug off these violations as no big thing, but the employee culture is listening now and it wants acknowledgment that you know you were wrong.

3. Show That You Mean It

Don't think that a simple apology gets you off the hook—that worked only when you were a manager. Do something a little exaggerated to make sure your people know that you know that you violated trust. Missed a promised meeting? Grab them, leave your phone on the desk, get in the car and take them someplace for a cup of coffee. Are you passing five free company coffeepots on your way to the car?

Sure, but this exaggeration is the stuff of cultural legends that will speak to your sense of accountability and the importance you place on integrity in your commitments.

▶ PASSION AND THE RATIONALE OF LOSING YOUR MIND

The myth of a manager is that they're a rock—a stable, stoic force amidst swirling seas of uncertainty. A leader isn't a rock; they're a rocket ship. A leader is a nutcase. You can't be achingly aware of your deepest personal values and obsessed with getting to a place you've never been to before and be a completely balanced individual.

You never want to be the one to trip the wire on a leader's vision: "I hear your values. I see your vision. I spit on these things." A leader isn't going to put you on Phase One of the disciplinary cycle; they're going to try to strangle you. Mess with Mother Teresa about taking care of those lepers and you would have been missing a few limbs yourself.

On the other hand, if you do something significant to promote their values and vision, well, you're still going to die but that's because they're licking you to death. Either way, you're going to get an exaggerated, emotional response—a passionate reaction.

Displaying this kind of personal passion can be a difficult concept to embrace. As a manager, you've been taught your entire career to give a dispassionate, logical response to emotional issues. The crazier things get, the calmer you're supposed to be. Leadership is different; the calmer things get, the crazier you should be, concerned that people aren't challenging enough obstacles on the way to your Better Place.

Fortunately, being somewhat of a nutcase about what you most believe in engenders trust in your leadership. People gain visceral proof that you really care about it.

This summoning of intense emotion might be uncomfortable for you as a manager, symptomatic of the same detachment that you've developed as protective cover. Maybe you fear you'll make yourself vulnerable by letting your emotions be easily triggered. Maybe you just prefer to keep a pretty even keel in life.

To keep your people's trust you may have to lose your mind, or at least appear to. "The great leaders have always stage-managed their effects," said Charles de Gaulle, and some of your passionate response may have to be calculated. So you tell yourself now anyway. If you're really sure about what you most believe in and somebody goes out of their way to provoke you or protect you, you're going to go out of your way to stomp or slobber them. It's instinctual.

▶ HOW TO DO IT

1. Positive Reinforcement

Can you name each of your employees' favorite flowers? Their favorite band? The upscale restaurant they most want to try? If each of your people could learn one new thing that wasn't related to work in any way, do you know what that would be? If they could spend a perfect day, do you know what that day would look like for each of them, from the time they got up until the time they went to bed? And why exactly should you care about any of these things?

Your people have just assumed a whole lot more importance in your life than they had before you decided to become a leader. They are now the people who can make or break your ability to meet your deepest values for at least half your waking hours. They will constantly be in a position to do this. What are you going to do for them?

As a manager, you may leave it to your company to handle the rewards; as a leader, it's up to you because it's about you. It's about your passion for supporting those who support your values and vision. It's no longer a matter of just celebrating what was done, but how it was done.

You don't have to throw a bunch of money at this. Even if you had the budget, the money often obscures the meaning, which is that you cared enough and knew enough to do something significant for them. The significance of material leadership reinforcement is in the obvious effort behind the reward. Don't buy them the cake; bake them the cake.

How do you find out what would be most meaningful to one of your people? Stay close to their world, care about them, listen to them and value them (aka leadership).

Here's something that will take no money at all. Is one of your people doing a great job at supporting your values and advancing the march to your Better Place? Stop and spend the time in your hectic day to handwrite them a letter. Explain that you know exactly what they've been doing and how moved you are by it, that it's this kind of effort that assures you that this Better Place will be achieved by the team. Mention that you just wanted to take the time to tell them how proud you are of their efforts and how much it personally means to you.

Mail the letter to their home.

Your employee gets home and is flipping through the mail. Magazines, bills, direct-mail offers . . . and a letter they didn't expect, with their company's name printed as the return address. Uh-oh. Worse than that, their manager's name is handwritten above it. UH-OH.

If they're living with someone, the value of your letter has just gone up 100 percent. "What's that, honey?" "Oh, nothing. Just a note from my boss telling me how they are *blown away by my fabulous work!*" Even if they just live with a pet: "Get your leash! We're going out!"

2. Negative Reinforcement

Your leadership vision is of obvious benefit to your people; why would someone deliberately violate it? The answer may be that they're testing your commitment to your vision. Don't resent them for this—considering what you're asking of them, they have the right to test it. Your biggest initial cynics will ultimately become your biggest converts—these are usually the people who have been searching the hardest for reliable inspiration and have been unable to find it.

You shouldn't violate common sense, human resources ethics or basic rules of effective confrontation, but you must show heat if someone disrespects your leadership, and it's got to be a special kind of heat. The kind that says, "You'll never see this reaction from me unless you step across this most important line."

SCREW IT UP

▶ MISTAKES: YOURS

Mistakes happen to everyone, even leaders. Especially leaders. It's the price leaders pay for boldly heading to someplace new when they don't have a clue about how to get there.

You are going to make mistakes in your transition to leadership. How could you not? Leadership is a lot of new behaviors, entered into at freeway speed, dependent on recently redefined relationships, often flying in the face of the way things have always been done and in the faces of the ones who have always been doing them. You won't have time to get your leadership right before you have to get it out there. Leaders develop in front of their followers—it's buried in the fine print of the job description.

Leadership is an equation for making mistakes.

On the bright side, if you don't screw up your first attempts at leadership, you're not doing it right. It means you're not moving far enough into new behaviors. You're not trying to get to a place that you've never been to before.

Only managers loathe mistakes; scientists, criminal attorneys and leaders actually find value in them. Leaders are obsessed with results, not blunders made in achieving them. They admit their errors to themselves and to others; this accountability is one of the unusual characteristics shared by all leaders. It's also one of the perks: Admitting your mistakes and learning from them is the best way to improve your chances of not making them again.

Leaders know that mistakes represent valuable information and that their vision and values matter more than an error in judgment. Since a leader is concerned only about achieving their vision, any information that helps them do it is good information—*"Oops, wrong road. Okay, we know that now. Let's get there a different way."* Yes, leaders actually talk to themselves like this. Don't be concerned: By the time this happens to you, you'll have something far more important to worry about.

THE FAR MORE IMPORTANT THING TO WORRY ABOUT

A Better Place based on the likes of Family, Integrity, Health, Freedom, Learning or Security? The big issue is not that your values and vision are going to be threatened—that will happen regularly. Your values are absolute concepts, and your pledge to get to the Better Place is an absolute commitment; it's tough to ensure they'll remain tamperproof within an organizational environment.

The big issue is whether, when they do get threatened, you're able to retain leadership credibility with your people. As long as the employee culture continues to trust you, it'll make sure you live to lead another day.

Fortunately your people aren't expecting you to be perfect as a leader. They'll forgive a lot of mistakes in the interest of your attempting to get them to a Better Place. What they are expecting is for you to be honest with them and committed to what you say you're committed to. You show you're honest by admitting what is true, even if it isn't good news. You show you're committed by refusing to abandon the principles of your leadership even when the pressure's on. Ultimately it's not a matter of making mistakes; it's a matter of surviving them.

▶ HOW TO DO IT

1. Never Lie to an Employee Culture

One reason leaps immediately to mind: You can't get away with it. Your employee culture has an unerring ability to tell if you really stand for what you say you do. Hell hath no fury like an employee culture scorned.

2. Pick Your Battles and Let People Know You Fought Them

An employee culture is realistic, and it knows you can't protect every threat to your values and commitment to the Better Place. But it wants to know you tried and is always up for a horrific story about the danger you incurred on its behalf.

3. Defend Your Definition, Not Your Value

Remember, your leadership is not based on the literal definition of a value; it's based on the transferable currency. Family doesn't mean time spent with family; it means open, honest communication and unconditional support—what that family time gives that makes it so important. If your *definition* of a value is under pressure, this is what you have to defend since this is what you used to create the promise of a Better Place.

4. React in the Name of Your Values

Let's stay with this Family example: You and your team are toddling affably along toward the Better Place when a directive comes along that is going to cause your people to work longer hours for the next six weeks, under extra pressure to perform and with less chance to be with their families—a clear violation of the leadership promise that everyone has embraced.

Say this to your people to preserve your leadership when faced with threat conditions:

"You know how committed I am to my values and to us getting to a Better Place. Now here comes this new announcement that messes with both. I have to tell you I don't agree with it and I pushed back on it, but this decision comes from a level above and cannot be changed. So I'm telling you that we're getting rocked on the way to our Better Place.

"Here's what we're going to do: We're going to rock it right back.

"First of all, we're going to come together like a family and bust out these new performance objectives better than any team in the company. Second, we're going to check to see if anybody on our team has a can't-miss family event during this period—anniversary or birthday, son's baseball game or long-held concert tickets. We'll put those things on the table and figure out how to make them happen.

"Not to be presumptuous, but I know you're going to be working some long, exhausting hours and won't have a lot of quality time to spend at home. I've taken the liberty of addressing a letter to your family thanking them for their support and I've enclosed a gift certificate for pizza and a movie for them to use one night when you can't be there to take them.

"Hear me on this: Most important is that we're going to act *like* a family during these tough times. It is absolutely okay to complain about this situation—all I ask is that you keep it here, in the family. During this time, I expect you to support one another and help everyone be successful. And we are not going to let the pressure turn us against one another. This family is going to protect itself and take care of itself."

● ● ●

The employee knows that you don't have control over every aspect of working conditions. When you respond in this way, people can be sure that when your leadership takes a direct hit, you refuse to abandon your commitment.

Mistakes may be valuable and survivable, but failures? Not so much in many corporate environments. What stops a mistake from becoming a failure is whether it's learned from, whether it's repeated and especially whether an employee culture decides to support its manager in the face of a wrong move.

MISTAKES: THEIRS

Now that you've gleefully given yourself license to make mistakes in the name of your leadership, your people need the same. You will have ignited their own efforts, and they'll be moving fast toward a place they believe is better for them. You need to make sure that they don't hesitate to go there for fear of making mistakes and you need to make sure their mistakes make them stronger.

Since you can't possibly be around for every choice your people will make, how do you ensure that they happen consistent with your most important values? How do you commit to supporting those choices without always knowing what they'll be?

► HOW TO DO IT

1. Turn Your Values into Rules for Living

Rules for living are simple "the way things are done around here" statements that become an operating guide for your people's independent judgment.

"I have Family as a value, so make the decisions you need to make. Just keep this in mind:

- Never put your job and your family into conflict without giving me the chance to do something about it.
- When you have knowledge about how to meet our goals, share it. When it's shared with you, consider it seriously even if you don't always agree with it.

- It's not a sin if you can't get something done. It is if you don't raise your hand to alert others and ask for help.

"I have Integrity as a value, so make the decisions you need to make. Just keep this in mind:

- Hold yourself accountable for your actions. Admit your mistakes when you make them and learn the lessons.
- No passive-aggressive behavior in this organization: Confront with respect but confront when necessary.
- Tell the truth, completely and on time.

"I have Spirituality as a value, so make the decisions you need to make. Just keep this in mind:

- You know that there is a right way to do business. Do business that way.
- Always treat one another with respect, as professionals and as human beings.
- Don't ever let your job pressure you to compromise ethics or personal standards. Let me know about it immediately if you think this is happening."

● ● ●

You will have translated your values into practical application, so any of your people can say, "How would my manager want me to do this?" Even if they go off the tracks, you'll know where it happened and you can reinforce their attempt to head in the right direction. If they've chosen to go in the wrong direction you can tie them *to* the tracks.

This is an easy process to manage, but leadership success depends on doing it consistently and with resolve. You're saying to your people, "Make any decisions you have to make, just do it according to these Rules for Living. If you make the wrong decision but follow these rules, I will back your play 100 percent because I'll know you were trying to do the right thing. But if you violate these simple guidelines, I'm holding you immediately and fully accountable."

You're making good choices their choice, which is a lot less complicated for both of you.

STEP FOUR: NOW, FIRST, NEXT AND LATER

Living your values at work. Emotional commitment. Leadership. These are complex issues. It wasn't my job to make them more complex; it was to make them achievable for you. Try them now and you'll find:

1. **You can do it.** You just needed urgent motivation and a reasonable tactical plan.
2. **It feels good to do it.** This is all about fulfillment of your deepest personal values.
3. **Your people will help you do it.** It's all about fulfillment for them too—the promise of vastly improved working conditions.
4. **Your company will allow you to do it.** Emotional commitment is what your company wants most from you. Once you start getting the results, you can count on the support.

▶ HOW TO DO IT

1. Commit to a Few Steps over a Few Weeks

As much as it pains me to say, the worst thing you can do is get giddily inspired by *Bury My Heart at Conference Room B*, proclaiming loudly to yourself and others that you will immediately embark on a series of massive behavioral changes. No doubt you will, and soon, but this is a process with new competencies and practices for you. They'll be new for the people you need to conspire with as well.

Start with the recommendations here. You'll be moving fast before you know it, but this way you'll be moving safely. And start soon, before the wind tunnel of your job picks you up and reorgs your attention span.

2. Confirm Your Values

This is the essential first step. Living your values will be a lot less compelling for you if they're not your values.

Use the methods in this book and don't be concerned if it takes a while. You are answering deep and complex questions for yourself. These methods are designed to guide you, but that doesn't mean it's going to come cheap and easy (yeah, yeah, unless those are two of your values).

You'll know it when you get there: You'll feel everything click into place and your motivation to pursue living them will be with you forevermore.

3. Take It Home

Start getting the support at home for what you're trying to do at work, and start getting the benefits too. Any fence between personal and professional fulfillment is a real dumb one: It hurts more than protects.

4. Make Sure You're Ready

As you plan on taking your values to the team, recognize that it will be one of the biggest commitments you ever make to other human beings. Don't consider asking for faith from them if you think you may default, or if your interest is casual, curious or unsound in its motives (work harder, not live better). Chew on it yourself before asking anyone else to swallow it.

5. Prepare Your Initial Declaration

When you are sure of your values, where they came from and how this can make life better for your people, it's time to prepare to declare it. Follow the guidelines in this book.

6. Get a Couple of Legends Ready

Before you even schedule the declaration meeting, be sure that you have a couple of cultural legends on the shelf, ready to go. Your people are going to be seeking confirmation of the claims you make in that talk, and the sooner you start providing them the better. Look for where the opportunities could come to reinforce, look for where the pressures could come to compromise. Provide them with rules for living so that you can respond in a legendary way.

7. Ease Off Yourself

This isn't about you; it's about you and your people, working together for something of mutual benefit. You don't have to do it all and you don't have to have all the answers.

STEP FIVE: WHO'S NEXT?

▶ TRANSLATING PROCESS AND PERKS TO YOUR PEOPLE

Bury My Heart at Conference Room B is about living your values at work by translating them into improved working conditions, thus generating your emotional commitment to the success of the company.

Not much in that sentence that wouldn't be good for your people to do too. You can help them do it, but it's not a matter of how; it's matter of when.

▶ HOW TO DO IT—AND WHEN

1. Build a Reliable Model

As mentioned some pages back, you won't be in a position to sanction this for your people until you've become skilled at it yourself. Skilled is going to require knowledge and experience, so it's going to take a while. And it's going to take motivation in its purest form for you to keep at it until you become expert. You must build the Better Place based on *your* personal values first, not theirs.

How long will this take? Not less than six months, maybe as long as a year. Get it right and get it tight. Trying to build leadership credibility a second time with the same team is doable but difficult.

You're not prioritizing your values over theirs because you're the manager; you're prioritizing building a stable process for everyone to live their own. Everyone will understand that this new commitment from you is a rewarding but daunting thing to build. It's fine to explain that it's going to take a while to get it right for everybody and that there's not much more that can be added to the to-do list, no matter how important.

2. Don't Discount What You're Providing

Not that there's anything wrong with a sack of potatoes, but you're not selling them one: You're doing a lot for your people by declaring your values and consigning them to building a Better Place to work. Beyond its obvious positive impact, you're providing the gift of the gods to your employee culture: Showing them what is most important to you is showing them how to get along in your world. Plus you're giving them all that leadership provides, such as unity of purpose and faith. This should more than hold them until you're ready for them to start on their own.

3. Be Clear about Their Responsibility

While you're developing your expertise, your team should be earning the right for their own values consideration by helping you and by taking care of the organization's business. Applying your values in a hosted environment—the company—implies a responsibility to perform at the highest level. The same will be true for your people when the opportunity comes.

4. Predict the Pressure

When you're ready to begin scaling this to your team, start by looking at where the difficulties will arise. There will be conflict between your values and theirs (but not as much as you might think since the transferable currency process is the great equalizer of values). There will be times when your people use their values as justification for petulant and self-serving points of view. There will be times when the business simply dominates any view of personal preferences.

Get the team together at the advent of introducing their own values involvement, forecast where the pressure could occur and develop plans to deal with it and promises not to let it panic people with the thought that this will never work.

5. Remember That You're Still a Manager

You'll still have management issues and you'll still have management accountability for your people's performance. There is nothing in this process that should prohibit or intimidate you from acting like a manager. Maybe the best manager they've ever had, though.

Because you're their manager, this is your environment as well as the company's. The team's responsibility is to support the values-based way in which you want people to work.

6. Do It Together

This has to be a collaborative process and it's a great one. The first step will be to help your people understand their individual values and what those values mean to them, then translating them to considerations of a Bitter and a Better Place. Next will come considerations of how their values will integrate with yours and with the demands of the business. Following that, agreements on how the values will be reinforced—monitored, supported, rewarded and addressed if not being upheld.

You will then be able to make the same What-How-Why deal as detailed in the next chapter. Living their values is a wonderful option for them, but since it's the source of their emotional commitment it's not going to be optional.

ORGANIZATIONAL IMPLEMENTATION

14

FIRST STEPS TO ENTERPRISE-WIDE RESULTS

Bury My Heart at Conference Room B is designed to work individually and produce individual manager results for the organization. The more managers who apply the process, the more the organization benefits.

To ensure enterprise-wide results, it has to be implemented enterprise-wide. The process works just as well, uses all of the same tactics, but requires additional processes and resources to institutionalize behavior on this scale. When senior teams contemplate it, this is the part that usually seems most burdensome. That they have to model the behaviors themselves is the part that usually seems the most worrisome.

It's not simple to do, but it's certainly achievable, as are the results. As is the personal fulfillment opportunity for every manager, at every level. It would double the size of this book to detail every step to enterprise-wide implementation, but here are all of the essential considerations.

► HOW TO DO IT

1. Embrace the Business Case

A company renowned for its customer experience doesn't consider it an add-on to their business, vulnerable to changes in strategic direction. It is embedded in the go-to-market model. The same must be true for the manager experience in your company if you are planning on this process to produce organizational results. It can't be started, then defaulted on, and so it should be initiated only after a deep commitment has been made to make it part of the way the business operates.

Anything this big will initially require regular proof of concept— by the company to the company. You should attach it to as many key business metrics, goals and targeted wins as possible. Whatever performance improvement demands increased manager productivity, unity and care for your company's success is a valid measurement for *Bury My Heart at Conference Room B.*

Companies whose revenues depend on recruiting and retaining top manager talent have long considered being known as a "best company to work for" a key performance metric. Use any such measurement of the organizational health of your manager population, or conduct engagement surveys that probe managers' ability to protect and apply their own values at work and how that affects their performance and that of their teams.

There should be a direct translation to the retention of top management talent, especially noticeable anytime that bonuses are unavailable and options are underwater.

Track also the ease of recruiting top talent. The best managers can get the best money, titles, job descriptions and geography from other firms, but they can't easily get a priority placed on their personal values. If your company is growing through acquisitions, measure your ability to stop the best managers from fleeing out the back door as you're coming through the front, due to your special reputation for encouraging manager fulfillment.

If the enterprise is seeking initial justification for systemic commitment to the process, let's say your managers were more satisfied, felt safer and so cared more about keeping the company safe. It's not too big of a stretch to imagine reduction in HIPO churn, an increase in breeding of the next generation of managers from within, managers' rapid acceptance of change, their improved unity and focus around goals, their reluctance to waste company resources and a lessening of pressure to constantly sweeten their compensation or have them turn sour on you.

The breakdown in strategic success is often in the handoff to a company's management population, which isn't fully committed to implementation. That's where *Bury My Heart at Conference Room B* started, in large companies frustrated by their inability to execute strategies. Yet these companies employed some of the best management teams in the world, who were already committed in every noticeable way. Financially, they were living the life of the rich and heinous. Intellectually, the environments were breathtakingly stimulating—Gunfight at the IQ Corral. Physically, offices were lit up like Christmas every night, including Christmas night. The only thing missing was emotional commitment, the most valuable kind of all.

Poor manager performance doesn't sink companies; poor manager behaviors do. The best manager behaviors, like emotional commitment, are sustainable only if the motivation for them is sustainable. The company can't keep up: The motivation has to be self-sustainable.

The opposite of rational is irrational, not emotional. Emotion in the human brain is a highly rational process, capable of producing wonderful irrational acts like passionate protection of a company. Your managers may protect their company now but not anywhere near as much as they protect themselves within the company. Implementing *Bury My Heart at Conference Room B* means you're not forcing them to prioritize. You're allowing their protective actions to be one and the same.

There is nothing vague about *Bury My Heart at Conference Room B* when it comes to driving business results. By embracing the process, your company is making a decision about what is best required to compete in the marketplace. However, you are also making an enterprise commitment that your company wants to take its sense of self—your confidence, your bragging rights—from how it acquires unparalleled devotion from its managers. This is as deep and necessary a commitment as linking it to specific metrics impact.

2. Reinforce the Right

If financial rewards or career advancement reinforcement ignores the importance of managers' personal values, they'll take the cue that the company commitment isn't real. Whatever systems provide financial reinforcement for performance should include the application of individual values as one of the criteria. Rewards should be linked not only to what was achieved but how it was achieved—using values and demonstrating emotional commitment.

3. React to the Wrong

There will be organizational temptation to compromise the process. There will be disbelievers who find it inappropriate, are too impatient for results or are so emotionally detached they can't envision such a transformation. There will be a manager culture that tests the company's support by disobeying and observing the reaction.

The reaction has to be swift and significant: Enterprise dedication to a certain treatment and expectation of your managers is not something to be messed with. It is not something to be tolerated because someone happens to generate a lot of revenue, is popular or iconic. As you prepare for implementation, prepare for where the pressure will fall and prepare an unwavering response to anyone who might doubt that their disregard would trigger consequences.

4. Don't Overpromise

As you implement *Bury My Heart at Conference Room B* throughout the organization, there will be conflicts, there will be mistakes, there will be misses and the company will not have all the answers about how it's going to happen. Fortunately you don't have to have all the answers and you don't have to solve all the problems yourself. This is about real leadership.

Your managers want to see the company and executive team demonstrate leadership behavior here, including the organizational transformation from managing manager fulfillment to leading it. If this means struggling with some of the new behaviors required, that's okay—you lose nothing by revealing the difficulty of embarking on something this important, of this benefit for your managers and their company. The more difficult it is, the more courage and commitment you're demonstrating by tackling it and getting tackled.

5. Announce the Organizational Demand

If your company is willing to make the investment in creating this opportunity for your managers, it should be made clear that it's an opportunity but it's not optional. Failure to adopt the practices that allow them to live their own values at work means less fulfillment for them, which the company doesn't want. Failure to live their own values means they won't bring their emotional commitment to their jobs, which the company won't allow.

Why in the world would any manager reject such an opportunity? Managers are often surprisingly reluctant to embrace personal fulfillment as a priority over professional success and consider the two concepts disconnected. They've been raised to take care of their company before taking care of themselves and have adjusted to whatever rewards and risks this entails.

Before the company can demand they pursue living their own values, it has to make the link to performance—give both a personal and professional reason for considering new behaviors: the What-How-Why Connection. This is best made by each member of the executive team to their own organization.

WHAT

Start by reminding managers of the performance or strategic goals of the business for the next year:

"Here is WHAT we have to accomplish in the business. Could anything possibly be more important than this?"

HOW

Talk about your own values and how they will define the character of your organization. This is your full leadership declaration—your top three values; your Moment of Truth story about how you know at least one of them is real to you; how they translate to the Bitter Place (current unsatisfactory state) and the Better Place (how good life could be) for the organization; that it's important to move from bitter to better (significance), that it takes a special group of people to do it (belonging) and that those people have to have certain qualities to make it happen (self-worth).

"Yes, there is one thing and that is HOW we accomplish it. Let me explain my own values to you and what that means to all of us—goals will come and go; how we live here is what will remain."

WHY

This is where you connect your first message about performance to the importance of your managers becoming emotionally committed. You are providing them with an entirely new reason for performing better.

"Could anything be more important than how we do what we have to do? Yes, that is WHY we have to do it—so you can live your own values at work. As long as we're on our game, accomplishing what we have to accomplish, I have more flexibility in our working conditions, including making sure you are allowed to live your values. It's only when the pressure increases because we're not taking care of the business drops that things get crazy, everybody gets micromanaged and we don't have as much control over how we want things to be. Take care of the business and I'll support you living the way you want to at work."

• • •

THE SECOND GREAT CZECH REVOLUTION
true tales from the *bury my heart* files

Communism officially fell in Czechoslovakia on November 28, 1989. The country promptly installed a fiery ex-poet as president, then scrambled to catch the rest of the free world in everything from political infrastructure to consumer technology. The new government invited two huge European providers—Eurotel and T-Mobile—to institute reliable cell phone service. Only when those were well established did it finally open up the possibility of a third license to a small operator. Ten years later, in November of 1999, tiny Oskar Mobil was born.

From the beginning it was clear that Oskar was the little company that could. Could quickly go out of business.

By the time Oskar got rolling, there was near total product penetration countrywide—everyone already had a cell phone and a service provider. Forget about growth; to even stay alive, Oskar couldn't make market share, they were going to have to *take* it and they were going to have to hold on to it. Take it from the biggest possible competitors already locked in snarling, snapping battle. "Good luck with that," the local business press said. "You're not going to make it."

It doesn't get lonelier than a Czech parking lot at 5:01

"Maybe they're right," sighed Oskar CEO Karla Stephens, staring once again at the company's nearly empty parking lot. Stephens is a natural business builder, fevered with the passion of the entrepreneurially possessed. Ordinarily prone to futurism, not fatalism, she was unusually worried. "We were in this temporary building. A few of us would work all day and night but at five o'clock everybody else was gone. How can you build a company like that? You've got to believe in the business after hours, not just nine to five. We had hired all these people and we needed their commitment. We weren't getting it and we didn't have time to wait for it."

"Karla was right about the time," confirms Al Tolstoy, president of TIW, the main Oskar shareholder. Al generally plays calm circuit breaker to Karla's live-wire act but is no less intense and in this case was no less

concerned. "We had to shake up the market so people would pay attention to us—do something dramatic. We had a lot of ideas but we needed
the ability to execute. Everything was going to come down to people. We
needed to take manager engagement to an entirely new level."

Quest for fire

Karla summoned Regina Miller, Oskar's VP of human resources. "I
said, 'Reg, we need a Big Idea. Go out there and find it!'" Regina rapidly
set off like the errant knight in a fairy tale—searching the world over
for a magic antidote as her queen and the kingdom wither away from a
mysterious illness. This was no fairy tale: The mysterious illness was low
manager commitment, and Regina Miller was a sophisticated manager
herself, with big enterprise experience. She wasn't easily bluffed and knew
she'd recognize the cure if she found it.

"I found it," recalls Regina. "I rushed back to Prague and I'm like, 'Oh
my God, look at this! It's called *Bury My Heart at Conference Room B*. It's
very different, Karla. It's the Big Idea!'"

The fuse is lit. And glued onto managers.

"I got *Bury My Heart at Conference Room B* right away," says Karla. "It
had been really frustrating not to be able to communicate to my executive
team what was important to me. I wanted profits but I wanted creativity
and wasn't willing to give an inch on either. And they were going, 'There's
just no pleasing her!'"

"The minute she got it, we all got it," recalls Regina. "The executive
team understood what was going on for her as a leader, and what her
values were. It immediately gave us the context for what she was trying to
do for us, creating the organization and building Oskar. We knew this was
the answer. Now we had to roll it out to our managers."

More like steamroll it: They brought *Bury My Heart at Conference
Room B* to every manager. They added it to the managers' Performance
Management Process—drilled fulfillment of personal values ("identifies
and understands own values; behaves in a way consistent with one's
own values; weighs own, others' and organization's values to guide

actions") right into the center of ongoing objectives and linked manager compensation to it. Next came "Values Week," focused on ensuring that every Oskar employee was familiar with their manager's values. Then they stepped it up to the employees themselves: Karla and her executive team hit the road to discuss the importance of personal values with the entire organization. The company began to survey managers and employees about whether they felt able to live their values on the job. And they encouraged people to talk about their values with customers—on the phone, in meetings, in the Oskar retail stores.

Oskar published a lavish hardcover book for its people about what it means to be an employee—and what your own values mean to Oskar. The message was not that everybody had to have the same values but that they had to have *some* values and they had to bring them to work.

It was a hard message to ignore. "Especially when I surprised the executives and redecorated all their offices by painting their values on the wall," says Karla. "Every time you went into somebody's space you would know what their values are and you could keep that in mind."

"Okay, I went a little crazy, but when I believe in something I believe in it," laughs Karla. "You know—this is a true story. And I forgot about it—somebody just brought it up the other day with me, and I was howling. When I lived in Prague, we had a house team. We had our driver, and we had women that helped with the house, and we had the nanny. I took them away for the weekend and did *Bury My Heart at Conference Room B* with them! But you know what? They didn't speak English at all and I didn't speak fluent Czech, so I had to translate the meaning of the values. I know, I know, but it gets even better, because I insisted that they each had to paint a picture to reflect their values, and those were in our house."

"Pretty soon people had absorbed the language of *Bury My Heart at Conference Room B*," says Regina. "The executive team's plan was to embed it in everything, coordinate it with everything, synch it with everything."

From the Oskar book:

Whatever future we have at Oskar is a future that has to include the real you. The real you is irreplaceable. There is no one else like you. No one else has the exact combination of values that you have.

No one else can make your specific and unique values come alive like you can. No one else can become the best you that there is. Only you can do that.

You alone are responsible for living your values everywhere and always. We can help by creating a values-based workplace, by encouraging you to share your values with us, and by respecting and supporting those values at Oskar. But ultimately it's up to you.

After all, they're your values and it's your life. Don't you want to be someplace where you can be the real you? What we need is that special combination that is you to make Oskar a place where we can all succeed. So bring your greatest asset, bring your values. Bring your special combination and unlock it—because when you reveal your values, the treasures hidden inside you won't be tarnished or disappear, but instead, will sparkle and glow.

"Czech managers all understood the freedom of the West," explains Al, "but they had no way of figuring out how to do that on their own. And so at Oskar, we swung open the door. We were saying you can have freedom but it comes with accountability. You have to stand up and be counted."

"It shook everyone up," remembers Regina. "We were clearly obsessed."

Preaching to the genetically reluctant

So much for the believers, but what about people paid to be professional skeptics? Were Oskar's board and majority investors growing concerned with this mania about incorporating personal values as a platform for corporate success?

"We used managers' values fulfillment as a key performance indicator for the business," explains Karla. "Any decision or action, we mapped back so our stakeholders could see the connection. But before that we took everyone personally through the whole process. We introduced *Bury My Heart at Conference Room B* to our board members, to our major investors and to our critical strategic vendors. We did a lot of reportouts to shareholders, and we did their values too. One year I did a photo album for each of our directors and started the first page with their values. Everyone was really excited."

"Everyone was really excited about the numbers," asserts Al. "And what happened is quarter over quarter, we began to grow, eventually at one point even faster than our two big competitors."

"If we weren't performing, they would have wondered," agrees Karla. "I remember talking about the implementation of *Bury My Heart at Conference Room B*, and Mike Hannon, our lead investor from the New York office of J.P. Morgan, kept asking, 'How are you going to sustain it? How are you going to see the results? How are you going to know it's working?'

"We already had a lot of great stories about how it was working, what people were doing in the business and what was happening differently as a result. We exceeded projected results for twenty-six straight quarters. Not only were we producing these financial results, [but] *Bury My Heart at Conference Room B* was [also] giving us manager loyalty and employee retention. Oskar was voted a highly desirable place to work and the most progressive firm in the entire country.

"I really believe the biggest thing it provided is confidence to the management team that they could lead the business. When you come out clean and say, 'This is who I am, this is what makes me who I am,' you find people embrace it. You go, 'Actually, I'm doing okay. I can do this and it's going to be okay.'"

The right thing to do

"I didn't know *Bury My Heart at Conference Room B* was going to stick so well and be so effective, but I knew we desperately needed something like it and I'd never seen anything like it," remembers Al.

"There is nothing like it," says Regina.

"There were a lot of things done right in the Oskar business," she continues. "Our brand focus, we were driven by passion, had a continuing emphasis on quality and we tightly controlled the margins. But this process allowed our managers to move fast and sure because they had context—they could understand the values of the person they were reporting to. It went all the way to the executives who now understood the way Karla wanted us to be as a team, her expectations for us as leaders in the business. We knew the kind of company that we were there to build. In the context of an organization with its own set of values, we all had individual values and were allowed to live them. Oh, yeah. We knew it was the right thing to do."

Let us not ever confuse right with easy

"Some people tried to use it against us," recalls Karla. "Older Czechs freaked out. They didn't think it was appropriate in the workplace. Plus we got tested all the time, but that didn't threaten me at all. It made my life easier. 'How can we trust you when you say creativity is a value and you are telling us to cut costs?' So I would say, 'Okay, you know what? The unfortunate part is that values do come into conflict. This is a situation that maybe isn't in conflict because if we don't make our numbers you'll have no chance at all to be creative.'"

"Ultimately we moved right through that," says Regina. "We were saying, 'This is our path. You can get on it quick, you can get on it in the middle, you can kind of get on it last, but if you don't get on it, you've gotta go.' All the key players stayed."

"It was easier for me with the executives," says Karla, "because I'd be like, 'Don't be scared to be real. Embrace the whole journey and the process. You'll be surprised how much more you can love your job and start to appreciate the people around you more. Really, be a little bit brave with the whole thing.'

"Sure was a lot of energy, though. Not just the work of actually implementing it but the emotional work. Implementation of *Bury My Heart at Conference Room B* requires constant vigilance and constant self-vigilance."

"Many times companies won't have the energy to keep pushing through the pushback and stay focused on execution," adds Regina. "That's what we did at Oskar."

Still, definitely the right thing to do

Karla: "We created an organization that was not scared. Think about that." Al: "You've got to create your own pulse. You've got to start your own movement." Regina: "Once it became clear that Oskar was not going to be stopped, other companies tried to replicate what we were doing. But you can't replicate a heartbeat. When you're building organizations, you want people to have great career experiences. And I think that's what we did for everybody in the company. I think we gave everybody an amazing career experience."

"Me included," says Karla. "And this was the catalyst. *Bury My Heart at Conference Room B* has a really big place in the story of this company. It was a pivotal part in the transformation of the business, especially at the executive level."

"It was the taking-off point," confirms Regina. "It was like a trajectory, if you were looking at a grid, right? We were a start-up, start-up, start-up and then *Bury My Heart at Conference Room B*."

Most definitely the right thing to do

On June 1, 2005, ClearWave, the subsidiary of TIW, which owned both Oskar and, in Romania, Connex, was bought by Vodafone. In breaking the news, London's PR Newswire–First Call described Oskar as "the fastest-growing operator in the Czech Republic."

Vodafone paid $4.4 billion.

YOU MUST
REMEMBER THIS

15

"THIS SHOULD BE a pamphlet," I mentioned back when we started, considering how incontestably valuable your emotional commitment is. Of course you want maximum career success, but if not living your values to the fullest is the cost, everyone is lost. Not only you, but your people, your company and the people outside your company who depend on its basic humanity.

All these pages later, I hope I've been able to build the case for why this is such a surprisingly complex issue to unravel and so why it had to be a book.

It has to be a book you believe in and will implement. Here, then, is the closing argument, delivered on behalf of your personal fulfillment, your success and the success of your company.

THE PURPOSE

▶ A COMPANY MUST LET MANAGERS LIVE THEIR VALUES

People are hesitant to embrace any world that is barren of what feeds them.

❖

It's impossible for your company to get what it wants most if managers have to make a choice between their own values and company priorities—even if they choose in the company's favor.

❖

A company may get strong manager performance regardless, and it may seem like emotional commitment. It's not. Financial, intellectual and physical commitment combine to masquerade as the missing type. Emotional commitment comes from a different place—stronger, deeper and far more dependable.

▶ LIVING YOUR VALUES IS THE KEY TO WORK/LIFE BALANCE

If you're not living your values at work, you're not living them in life.

❖

The detachment danger may not be in your ride to work but in the ride back home. You can't turn your values on like a garage door opener when you pull into the driveway at the end of another enriching day of meetings.

❖

Work/life balance isn't just about where you spend your time; it's about *how* you spend your time. It's about getting the essence of what your family, friends and personal priorities give you, no matter where you happen to be.

▶ YOUR LEADERSHIP IS IMPORTANT

Your company is not a passive environment. It has its own purpose, priorities and life force. Living your values in such an environment cannot be a passive process.

❖

A leader is the conduit for their cause. The cause is fulfillment of their own values.

❖

As a leader you will transform your values into purpose and connection for your people. Our humanity cannot be self-proclaimed. It is activated only when we offer it to others.

▶ YOU SHOULD LIVE YOUR VALUES AT WORK

Your values are your essence: an undistorted mirror showing you at your pure, attractive best.

❖

There is no finer feeling than being warm inside when it's cold outside.

❖

This is your one and only precious life. Somebody's going to decide how it's going to be lived and that person had better be you.

THE PATH

There is a road.

It is the road that every renowned leader in history has walked down to achieve success. When you strip the mystery and mythology out of leadership, it is a specific series of tactical steps, often performed in a specific order and always for a specific reason.

This is not some marbled corridor of privileged power. Think of it instead as a dirt road, hot and dusty, lined with sunbaked, gnarled trees on one side, half-buried railroad tracks on the other. It is a humble path that has seen greatness and waits with patient certainty to see it again.

When you finish this book, you will have started on that road, for each of those leaders has done the same things that you just learned to do.

From a world of possibilities you picked the values most important to you. You dug deep into your life to understand why those values are so important. You translated your values into the promise of better conditions for others to get their attention and you described intolerable current conditions to create the conflict that sparks action. You gave people something along the way to a Better Place by focusing on what is sure to be most deeply satisfying to them. You learned how to protect leadership credibility when your values and vision came under pressure and how to reinforce it—positive, negative, up and down. You learned how to turn mistakes into momentum and how to create the conditions that allow your followers to do the same.

And you didn't wait for anyone to let you do it.

If you have ever revered any of the greatest leaders in history—shook your head in wonder at their character and achievement—understand that your footsteps are now planted firmly in the dirt, right next to theirs. You can look back over your shoulder and see where you've come from. When you implement what you now know about leadership—exactly how and exactly why—you'll move all the rest of the way down that road, to the fulfillment, impact and legacy that await you.

Keep walking, my friend. You're on the right road.

THE WHOLE POINT

For yourself, because your life is happening to you right now and you do not get the time back that you're spending at work. For your family, because the health of your family outside the job depends in part on the health of your family inside the job. For your people, because it's not easy working in environments of constant uncertainty and pressure for someone you only know as "my manager." For your customers, because people don't trust companies; they trust people. For your company, because it's not a product or services company; it's a human company selling products or services and the pivot point upon which any strategic success rests is the discretionary effort of its human organization.

And for the world, because, let's face it, things are very weird out there right now and we have every indication that they're going to get a whole lot weirder before they get any better.

What is it that any manager can do about the conditions that affect the world at large? You can fall back to your own community—not just the one chosen by you outside the job but the one assigned to you inside the job—and in the name of what you know to be right, start by making that world a Better Place. Can one manager really change the world? Considering the state of the world today, that's the only way it can change—one person influencing one group of people at a time.

For all of these reasons, I urge you to . . .

Be human first. A manager second.

They cherish each other's hopes.

They are kind to each other's dreams.

—HENRY DAVID THOREAU

PART 5
UNDER THE HOOD

If Passion drives,

let Reason hold the reins.

—BENJAMIN FRANKLIN

FOR MORE ABOUT
BURY MY HEART
AT CONFERENCE ROOM B

For information on the enterprise consulting solution, training program and keynote speech versions of *Bury My Heart at Conference Room B*, check out my company's Web site, slapcompany.com. While you're there you can get plenty of additional information about this book, post your comments and questions and engage in real dialogue with other real managers, many of whom also believe their desks appear to be melting.

To contact me directly, it's stan@burymyheart.com. I'd be honored to hear from you.

"ACKNOWLEDGMENTS"
DOESN'T SAY ENOUGH

Looking Back at Twenty Years of Help Along the Way

There is a difference between good and the best of anything. Best is a complex alchemy of higher purpose, personal standards and passionate obsession. The people who have helped this book come into existence are the best.

At first, all the way back, even before the initial research, I made the whole thing up. From my own experience as a manager and management consultant the concept of *Bury My Heart at Conference Room B* seemed intuitively right. Testing it with managers and their companies seemed to confirm this—they loved it and it was getting great results. So too did my first research, which was mostly used to deconstruct leadership. But *Bury My Heart at Conference Room B* has always been a free-range beast. It soon matured into a far more complex set of arguments and issues around emotional commitment and values that centered on how the brain chooses to work in organizational environments. You can't make *that* stuff up, but of course I did.

Enter Dr. Julia Shumelda, with her subspecialty in psychoneuro-biology, in 2002. We were recommended to each other and I invited her to witness a *Bury My Heart at Conference Room B* session, thinking, "Uh-oh, it all ends right here; maybe none of what appears to be working really works." One of the more gratifying moments in the early development of this process was receiving the first couple hundred pages of research documentation from Julia proving that it all does—leading to the unofficial slogan in my company: "Born of ignorance, backed by science." Dr. J. is part of the slap company now, although I always advise people not to make direct eye contact with her. She appears as an innocent doe sniffing your essence but will have your neocortex spliced, diced and served with pickles before you realize it's missing. Julia's limitless humanity, intelligence and devotion have deepened and brightened this work throughout, and it is as much embedded in her as it is in me.

Through Julia I got Brad Nelson, now an EVP at the slap company and a most righteous cat. *Bury My Heart at Conference Room B* went to work on him and he on it, exposing it to his unyielding standards of integrity and impact, tirelessly fine-toothing the manuscript, researching various critical support points and attempting to penetrate the labyrinth of James Brown's estate for usage rights to the lyrics of "I Feel Good." If you can judge your own quality and character by the quality and character of those who choose to associate with you, I am an amazingly smart and soulful guy.

The research team for this book numbered twenty-three people including Pulitzer winners and ace investigative journalists plus the aforementioned Julia and Brad. Leading the search to unearth the hidden and open the closed were Patrick Dillon, Pete Henig and Dan Starer (of Research for Writers). Delos Knight, fact-checker extraordinaire, came out of retirement on a mission to save me from personal and professional humiliation only to discover that it's apparently more of a journey than a destination. The wonderful Rob Bogosian did the second round of research into the science of leadership in organizations and was kind enough to discuss some of it with me very, very slowly on writing days when I'd had thirty minutes sleep. Alexis Phillips at TCI is an expert psychometrician; she gave of herself selflessly to explore the book's diagnostics and I selfishly accepted. Fred Arnstein knows a disturbing amount about statistics and surveys, and his incisive opinions helped make the book better.

Brenda Segal at HarperCollins is a friend who first suggested the name of superagent Margret McBride. One of the FAQs on the McBride Literary Agency Web site addresses when someone can expect to hear back directly from Margret after submitting an unsolicited manuscript—the answer is basically, "Don't wait up." She was on a plane to see me the week she received mine, and we embarked upon a nine-year relationship that has been mostly characterized by my many "I'll have the book done soon" and "What I meant by 'soon . . .'" e-mails. Early on she said to me, "I've been waiting my whole career for you." Likewise, I'm sure, Margret. It's a shivering delight to watch you do your thing, and your unwavering faith in me gave me faith in myself when I needed it the most. Thanks also to your fine team including Donna DeGuitas, Anne Bomke and Faye Atchison.

So I tell Margret that I only want my books in the hands of someone who gets it. Who gets what's needed to change companies and those who manage them. Who gets what's really at stake for us all if this change doesn't happen. She says, "You've got to send the proposal to Adrian Zackheim at Penguin/Portfolio." "Yeah, okay," I say. *"Now,"* she says. Adrian and his team radiate competency. I'm from California and have an allergic reaction to the word "awesome," but there isn't a better one to describe this group. Special thanks to Courtney Young, Will Weisser, Allison McLean, Fred Huber, Kent Anderson, Phil Budnick, Glenn Timony, Katya Shannon, Nicholas LoVecchio, Joe Perez, Amy Hill, Pauline Neuwirth, Veronica Windholz, Laura Clark and Emily Angell.

I am humbled and inspired by the people who allowed me to tell their very personal stories in this book: Orlando Ayala, Mike DeCesare, Rick Devenuti, Adrian Jones, Iin Nugroho, Janet Rolle and Mike Spence. Four other people gave me stories that, much to my embarrassment, I couldn't figure out how to get in the book: Greg Dowling, Kip Knight, Bruce Lee and Trenton Truitt had much to tell you, with much power and beauty.

Thank you to those who willingly flung open the doors to their companies and hearts, including: Harold Bronson, Richard Foos, Gary Stewart and Chris Tobey (RIP) from Rhino; Regina Miller, Karla Stephens and Al Tolstoy from Oskar; Michael Ziegler and the people from PRIDE; Tom Quadracci and the people from Quad/Graphics; and the fine and patient folks at SAS and also at Progressive Insurance, the latter of which, while I didn't include it in the book, is a story worth telling about a great company.

I have my own company—called slap, by a remarkable coincidence— and it is constantly busy, absorbed in deep enterprise strategic work and conducting training sessions around the planet. Completing the book took me away from the company on a regular basis and the people there stepped in to fill the vacancy without hesitation or complaint. Thank you to all the great folks at slap for keeping the wheels on, and especially to Mikki Laurel, John Morrella, Mark Sato, Paul Sherman, Robby Testa and Joel Yanowitz. The book's done everybody and I'm back—pretend like that's a good thing. Also a shout-out to Laurel Dunn, who, as Laurel Phillips, kept it going at the beginning. I swore back then that—well, I swore back then, period—I would never forget you and I never have.

This book was road tested for many, many years in days-long sessions with fine people doing the tough job that managers do. I thank all of you and remember many of you, especially you, Ava Denton, the *Bury My Heart at Conference Room B* poster child. Thank you to all of my company's clients, smart and, in the early days, fearless, who got it right away and wanted it for the enterprise and for their managers. Special thanks to Rosie Andrews, Sharon Foster, Barbara Gordon, Kathleen Hogan, Derek Ingalls, Pieter Knook, Sandra McDevitt, Sanjay Mirchandani, Ben Putterman, Bruce Wilson, Liz Wiseman, Terri Wolfe and Lori Wong for support at key stages. Gary Stewart: to answer your question, this is how long it took.

Constant believers who have urged this work on also include Mike Cowman, David and P. J. Jamison, Greg LeClair, Ron Luyet, Kathy Myers and Dean and Cheryl Radetsky. Back in the day, thanks to Rex Brown, Tony Martinez and Dan Terry. Thank you to Rebecca Derminer, the gracious and dedicated widow of MC5's Rob Tyner, and to Wayne and Margaret Saadi Kramer for their support. Check out the Kramers' fine charitable foundation, Jail Guitar Doors (jailguitardoors.org), which operates in the Wayne Kramer tradition of merging the power of music with fierce social conscience.

A lot of the people mentioned here read and commented sagely on various drafts of the book, as did Denise Andrews, Dr. Allen Answorth, Heidi Brandow, Sue "Birdi" Burish, TJ DiCaprio, Mimi Mehrabi, David Ranzer (RIP), Phil Rogers, Nina Simosko, Denmark West and Mike Yoffie. I took all of your comments seriously, especially the positive ones. Thanks to all the busy managers who took the time to answer the survey—I know your e-mail was breeding like rabbits while you were away. And a superspecial, deep, personal thanks to whomever I inevitably forgot to mention.

Jim Keppler and his team at Keppler Speakers Bureau have loved to claim I'm the only one of their keynote speakers who hasn't written a book. They arrange a lot of *Bury My Heart at Conference Room B* keynotes, so maybe they've been sending out IOUs in my name all these years. Thanks to Gary McManis, Joel Gheesling, John Turan, Kellie Skibbie, Eliot Gunner, Tonia Cleland, Jay Callahan, Bill Hallock, Chris Clifford and Jenny Thomas.

Thanks to Liz Hazelton and Mark Fortier for getting the story out. Also to the wonderful Kip Knight of KnightVision Marketing, who dragged me into social networking, and to Andrea Cherng, who is determined to keep me there, and to Dave Wallinga and TWG for the new Web site.

My extreme gratitude to the singularly fabulous Alayne Reesberg, who knows everybody who is anybody and whose heart is as big as her black book. Also to Rik Kirkland, a Southern gentleman of intelligence, wit and unimpeachable loyalty. I am impressed that I can call him my friend.

Not officially in the slap company but on my balance sheet as big assets are people who allowed me to focus on writing this book: Steve Berson, who keeps a hawkish eye on the state of the numbers and my mind; Judy Ranzer, who gets me in and out of every imaginable place as we take *Bury My Heart at Conference Room B* on multiple world tours; David Gorman and the Hackmart team, so good at what they do, and what they did for this book is much appreciated; Dr. Bill Grossman, wise and kind, who knows the ways of the heart better than most; Bob Christoph at Typo Finders, who has clearly named his company as a touching tribute to me; Lou Pappalardo at Northern Lights for hitting the presses whenever I pressed; Danya and Ivar at The Key Printing & Binding for holding on to the proposal for years and then rushing it in hours; David Moss of 24hourtek for instant support whenever the all-caps e-mails came screaming his way in the middle of the night; Andrew Tonkin for help wrestling that greased pig of a subtitle; Howard Rosenberg, who can make anyone look like a star; and KB Morrissey for transcribing various indecipherable interviews on nights and weekends, although I'm sure I didn't say half of those things.

The leadership portions of *Bury My Heart at Conference Room B* brought me into contact with a lot of information about history's greatest leaders. I found them to be real people after all, flawed in all the best ways. It made their accomplishments even greater.

I wrote this book in one of two modes: demanding absolute silence from those around me (*"Quiet!"*) or blaring my music as loud as possible (*"What?"*). I used two playlists, called Manic and Depressive, and I thank all of the artists who saw me through long days and bleary nights.

My lovely wife, Diane, has throughout manuscript completion been the Queen of Tolerance—a tiny country of which I am the only subject. She and I were ritualistically trudging out of yet another bookstore a few years ago, dragging fully loaded bags. "What sort of sick twist is this?" I asked her, considering we already have a library at home with over 5,000 titles. "Why do we keep buying books? It's like we're addicted to the process."

I finally figured it out: We both had kind of unsettling childhoods, and we both learned early on to read as an escape. No unhappiness could find us, lost between pages for hours or days. We're not kids anymore, and we're not unsettled, but that feeling has never left us. We're not buying books; we're buying safety and salvation and imagination of what's possible when the story is new.

I wouldn't dare to put myself in the same category as all the authors who have moved me so. But I think it's a lot of what has driven me to be one myself. Just the rare chance that I could do that for someone, for you, made all this worthwhile. Serious.

Sawyer Rocket: You make my heart sing. You make everything groovy.

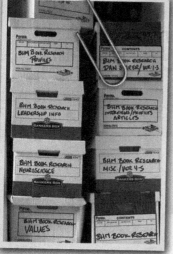

Excerpts from
Bury My Heart at
Conference Room B
Research Notes

No disrespect is intended by the title of this book to any American Indian tribe, past or present, or to the American Indian Movement.

On December 29, 1890, over 150 American Indians, primarily women and children, were massacred by U.S. armed forces at an encampment near Wounded Knee Creek, in South Dakota. This was a tragic but common occurrence; for years, Indians of all tribes had been abused, cheated and forced into desperate living conditions by the Bureau of Indian Affairs. The stated governmental policy was to "conform Indians to the white man's ways, peaceably if they will or forcibly if they must." Tribes were harshly relocated to areas where their known methods of hunting and gathering could not produce enough food. Children were mandated to attend schools that forbade traditional Native American culture and language.

The battle coincided with the Indian tribes' reinstatement of the Ghost Dance, a traditional sacred ceremony conducted in defiance of the government's Dawes Act, which had forced them to give up their spiritual practices. Ironically, the Ghost Dance was an attempt by tribal members to reverse the conditions contributing to their extinction by starvation—a quest to renew the earth, return the buffalo and bring back loved ones who had already perished. It was specifically a message of peace, imploring the tribes not to fight each other or the white man: "You must not fight. Do right always." Tragically it was declared an act of war by a government anxious about loss of control should Indians be allowed to pursue their deep personal priorities.

The American Indian Movement (AIM), whose slogan was "Remember Wounded Knee," was founded in 1968 to deal with rising unemployment, poor schooling and slum housing. Among other accomplishments, AIM opened its own schools and created a representative agency in cooperation with the United Nations.

On February 27, 1973, AIM occupied the original Wounded Knee site to protest extreme poverty and marginalization by the government and the Bureau of Indian Affairs. In the tradition of these sorts of things, it didn't go all that well.

→ INVENTED GHOST DANCE. NICE HAT.

In 1890, the Pine Ridge Lakota believed that the earth would surely be renewed the next spring. It was just the excuse they needed to ignore their Bureau of Indian Affairs agent, Daniel Royer, whose Indian name translated as "Young Man Afraid of Indians."

E: BURY MY HEART AT WOUNDED KNEE BY DEE BROWN
AMERICAN INDIAN MOVEMENT: AIMOVEMENT.ORG BUREAU OF
INDIAN AFFAIRS: BIA.ORG

". . . the ability to integrate one's experiences around a coherent and enduring sense of self lies at the core of creating a user's guide to life—an internal guidance system."

[Quartz, S. and Sejnowski, T. (2002). *Liars, Lovers and Heroes: What the New Brain Science Reveals About How We Become Who We Are*. New York: HarperCollins]

"God is a comedian performing before an audience that is afraid to laugh."
— Voltaire

"One form of emotional numbing that is widespread in our competitive culture is the tendency to compartmentalize our emotions . . . Many success-oriented people, fearing that their personal feelings will impede their upward climb, learn not to feel when they think it will get in their way.

[Steinberg, M. (2000). *The Stranger in the Mirror: Dissociation—The Hidden Epidemic*. New York: HarperCollins]

"IT'S JUST A JOB. GRASS GROWS, BIRDS FLY, WAVES POUND THE SAND. I BEAT UP PEOPLE."
— MUHAMMAD ALI

"THE LAST THING I WANT TO SAY IS 'I'M A VICTIM', BUT I AM. I BELIEVE IT'S A TRICKLE DOWN FROM GEORGE BUSH."
— COURTNEY LOVE

"[A study of] 120 records of schizophrenic patients admitted to the Ljubljana (Slovenia) psychiatric hospital between 1881 and 2000. . . revealed that paranoid delusions, feelings of persecution and the belief that someone is out to get you appear to be unique to the 20th century."

[Suddath, Claire (2008). "The Evolution of Insanity," *Time* Magazine]

TIME 88

"... the [detached] person may try to regulate emotional reactions by cognitively distancing himself from his feelings or the situation. Examples of such practices may be attempting to think of nothing at all, mentally switching off, waiting passively for something to change or engaging in the wishful thinking that things would be different."

[Lord, R., Klimoski, R. and Kanfer, R. (2002). *Emotions in the Workplace: Understanding the Structure and Role of Emotions in Organizational Behavior*. San Francisco: Jossey-Bass]

Family. Integrity. Health. Freedom. These are examples of values. If these are some of your own ... to compromise them in any way to do ... values at work. It's not a matter of yo ... relentlessly seductive forces being a ... create a sense of personal values fulfill ... rities in its place.

You can be a sm ... ily as a core value—and easily e ... your family so you can make a bunch of money to take care of your family by killing the com-

> **Some mornings it doesn't seem worth it to gnaw through the leather straps.**
> **—Emo Philips**

Financial rewards are still rewards and will produce good feelings in managers, including some dopamine reaction. But they are externally mediated and so they take work on the part of the company. The company has to align causes of neurochemical reaction with immaculate accuracy and consistency, or emotional commitment will vary and break down. If there is no bonus, if strategies don't make sense, if there's too much of a pull between work and something equally or more attractive outside of work, or if there is conflict with other dopamine-reinforced memories, things fall apart.

Emotional rewards are internally mediated, though, and there is an endless, predictable supply as long as managers are allowed to remain true to their own values. Commitment is then self-generated by the limbic system and all other kinds of commitment follow.

"Vitality is an abstract property which changes in response to organism experience."
[Anderson, J.J. (2000). *Ecological Monographs* 70(3): 445-470.]

"Conflict occurs when a person must choose between incompatible, or mutually exclusive, goals or courses of action. Conflict may also arise when two inner needs or motives are in opposition."

[Atkinson, Jan (2003). Excerpted from published notes of a lecture: Stress, Health and Coping, Psychology for Medicine course, Oxford University]

Plato founds the Academy in 367 B.C., Aristotle cuts the ribbon on the Lyceum thirty-two years later and it's start your limbic engines as Galeno races to first describe the anatomy of the brain in A.D. 170 and Avicenna is right on his heels with distinct cognitive processes like common sense and imagination, and let's leap to a four-digit year where in 1506 it's easy to sound hip at parties in Croatia if you use the term *psichiologia*, or "psychology," which Marulic has just originated but he's not partying down himself because it's all work, work, work with this guy as he publishes multiple mind-numbing volumes of *The Psychology of Human Thought* but at least the concept really catches on and is still the rage in 1635 when Neuhaus nails the first book about the reasons for studying psychology, giving inspiration to Locke and his *Essay Concerning Human Understanding*, while in Germany Thomasius cranks out a whole collection of recent proposals for a "new science for discerning the nature of other men's minds," and things are toddling along at a steady pace when—*wham, bam*—in 1732 von Wolff up and completes the first study of empirical psychology, after which Reid accepts the first Chair of Moral Philosophy in Glasgow and Cullen introduces the world to the term "neurosis," and things start really humming as the study of psychological behaviorism rears its troubled little head in the classical associationism of British empiricists like Hume, and now we're rockin' in the free world because in 1859 Bain releases *Emotions and the Will*, while in Japan Motora receives his country's first Ph.D. in psychology and, not to be outdone, Yougjing finishes the first Chinese translation of a Western psychology book (Raven's *Mental Philosophy*) while back in the States the two James pieces "What Is an Emotion?" and "The Stream of Consciousness" still top the psychology hit parade as the study of the mind moves from philosophical to experimental with Wundt and the first-ever psychological laboratory in Leipzig, after which they're springing up like chicken franchises in America, Italy, Russia, Canada, France, Belgium, Mexico, Holland, Romania, Austria, England and Poland in roughly that order, years before Freud finally gets around to rethinking the medieval work of Persia's Ibn Sirin and writes *The Interpretation of Dreams* and then *Psychopathology of Everyday Life*, blasting us into the twentieth century, which sees not only the establishment of fundamental tenets of behaviorism from the likes of Skinner, Rogers and Festinger in the 1950s, but the rise of cognitive science, embracing everything from philosophy and psychology to artificial intelligence, and the introduction of neuroscience, which blows everybody's minds, so to speak, with dramatic findings about biological and artificial neural networks, presynaptic neurotransmitter release rates and mossy fibers and, by 1998, voilà, you have over 1,700 people licensed to practice psychology in Paraguay and here come the writings of Damasio, Pinker, LeDoux, Rokeach, Csikszentmihalyi and Schore making knowledge of how and why the brain works accessible to anyone who has one, paralleling the exhaustively researched conclusions on self-based work motivational models in the 1960s of McClelland (1961), Rosenberg (1965), deCharms (1968), in the 1970s of Korman (1970), Gergen (1971), Katz and Kahn (1978), Cantor & Kilhstrom (1979), and in the 1980s of Azjen & Fishbein (1980), Brief & Aldag (1981), Gecas (1982), Schlender (1985), Bandura (1986), and Markus & Wurf (1987), but let's seal the records on personal motivational methods during those generally embarrassing decades since thankfully that's what the courts agreed to do for many of you and get right to Harvard's Beer & Katz study of 1998, which asked the seemingly rhetorical question, "Do Financial Incentives Work?" and proceeded to prove that they don't, and the non-calculative-based work behavior audits of Freeman in 2001 and Otto & Stephen in 2003, and finally just split the difference between Plato and today and say that the functioning of the human brain has been carefully analyzed for 1,000 years, which is 365,242 days and is also 8,765,808 hours, so the source of emotional commitment in managers is no longer a mystery since the total number of genes in a human being is now thought to be somewhat fewer than 25,000, meaning that humans are simpler than mustard weed, which is thought to contain 27,170.

Money can't buy you happiness but it can buy you a yacht big enough to pull up right alongside it.
—David Lee Roth

[Fig. 11]

"A hypothesis proposed by Dr. Terrence J. Sejnowski, a neuroscientist at the Howard Hughes Medical Institute and Salk Institute in La Jolla, California, is that the dopamine system evaluates rewards, both those that flow from the environment and those conjured up by the mind. When something good happens, the system releases dopamine, which, in essence makes the owner of the brain take some action."

[Blakeslee, S., "How the Brain May Weigh the World with Simple Dopamine," The New York Times, March 19, 1996]

"I FEEL GOOD, LIKE I KNEW THAT I WOULD"
—JAMES BROWN

". . . but with chronic cortisol exposure, dopamine production is curbed and the feelings of pleasure fade."
[Sapolsky, R., "Taming Stress," *Scientific American*, August 10, 2003]

"The mesolimbic dopamine system . . . seems to be ordinarily in play to provide a sense of pleasure in whatever people find rewarding, like sex or chocolate or a job well done," according to Dr. Annarose Childress, a neuroscientist at the University of Pennsylvania.
[Goleman, D., "Brain Images of Addiction in Action Show Its Neural Basis," *The New York Times*, August 13, 1996]

A 1999 Yankelovich Partners survey revealed that 29 percent of men and 8 percent of women believe that giving a box of chocolate as a gift will increase their chances of getting sex.

The survey ascertained that women prefer caramel centers while men prefer nuts.

VALUES ARE PHYSICALLY HARD-WIRED INTO YOUR NERVOUS SYSTEM. HAVING THEM IS NOT OPTIONAL. ONLY LIVING THEM IS.

"Recent findings obtained by recording EEG's from the scalps of volunteers . . . indicate that the cooperation between molecules of each hemisphere . . . shows that sensory and limbic areas of each hemisphere can rapidly enter into a cooperate state, which persists on the order of a tenth of a second before dissolving to make way for the next state. The cooperation depends on the entry of the entire hemisphere into a global chaotic attractor."
[Freeman, W.J. (2000), "Emotion Is Essential To All Intentional Behaviors", in M.D. Lewis & I Granic (eds.), *Emotion, Development, and Self-Organization: Dynamic Systems Approaches to Emotional Development*. Cambridge, UK: Cambridge University Press]

"The emotional, paleomammalian brain, or limbic system, wraps around the brainstem and modifies the instinctive behavior of the reptilian brain with actual experiences and the incorporation of feelings, emotions and memory . . . The limbic system powerfully tracks the external world and simultaneously modulates our internal physiology congruently. It stands at the crossroads of these two data streams: monitoring incoming information from our sensory experience and then up- or down-regulating our physiology accordingly. It is our visceral as well as emotional brain."

[MacLean, Paul (1990). *The Triune Brain in Evolution*. New York: Plenum Press]

"The emotional signal can operate entirely under the radar of consciousness. It can produce alterations in working memory, attention, and reasoning so that the decision-making process is biased toward selecting the action most likely to lead to the best possible outcome, given prior experience. . . ."

[Damasio, A. (2003). *Looking for Spinoza: Joy, Sorrow, and the Feeling Brain*. Orlando: Harcourt, Inc.]

"Information deemed life-threatening or self-preserving, of course, receives priority, as does information with strong emotional content, as the same pathways are used for both. Information threatening our survival is channeled *directly* to the amygdala taking a one-synapse, quick and dirty, emergency route, rather than taking a more leisurely pathway to the neocortex. Thus the amygdala can commandeer the neocortex by sounding a neural alarm, which then activates the fight/flight complex."

[LeDoux, Joseph (1992). "Emotion and the Limbic System Concept," *Concepts in Neuroscience* 2]

"Values are different states of intentionality that when activated guide behavior and create meaning. In preparation for the execution of intended action, the limbic system also includes states of emotion and effect that are implemented by the neuromodulatory nuclei of the brain stem."

[Freeman, W.J. (2000), "Emotion Is Essential To All Intentional Behaviors", in M.D. Lewis & I. Granic (eds.), *Emotion, Development, and Self-Organization: Dynamic Systems Approaches to Emotional Development*. Cambridge, UK: Cambridge University Press)]

"WE ARE THE BARTENDERS OF OUR OWN SOUL." —MICHAEL MURPHY

☺   Of the 36 alternatives, running away is best.   ☺

07 14 25 28 38 23 07

THE HUMAN BRAIN HAS CAPACITY FOR 60,000 WORDS. HERE ARE THE THREE THAT YOU NEED TO MOST KNOW: LIVE YOUR VALUES.

"Intentionality, whether conscious or unconscious, can be thought of as a value-driven selection directed towards a future goal."

[Modell, A. (2003). *Imagination and the Meaningful Brain*. Cambridge, MA: MIT Press]

"From modern neuroanatomy, it is apparent that the entire neocortex continues to be regulated by the paralimbic regions from which it evolved."

[Tucker, D. M. and Luu, P. (1998). "Cathexis Revisited: Corticolimbic Resonance and the Adaptive Control of Memory," *Annals of the New York Academy of Sciences* 843, pp. 134–152]

"When you get motivated in any significant way, it means the sub-cortical regions that connect with the amygdala have synchronized with each other. The neural networks in the limbic system, hypothalamus and brainstem start pulsing together, usually in the theta frequency of four to seven times per second . . ." (Kocsis and Vertes, 1994, Lewis, 2005)

"Meanwhile the supposedly irrational amygdala-based network helps construct your appraisals, values and strategies through its upward projection into the cortex."

[Hanson, Rick and Mendius, Richard (2009). *Buddha's Brain: The Practical Neuroscience of Happiness, Love and Wisdom*. Oakland: New Harbinger]

"I'D LIKE TO GET SOMETHING TOGETHER, LIKE WITH HANDEL AND BACH AND MUDDY WATERS, A FLAMENCO TYPE OF THING. IF I COULD GET THAT SOUND, I'D BE HAPPY."
— JIMI HENDRIX

"The latest research in neuroscience confirms that emotion and cognition can best be thought of as separate but interacting functions or systems, each with its own unique intelligence...the key to the successful integration of the mind and emotions lies in increasing the coherence (ordered, harmonious) function in both systems and bringing them into phase with one another. . . .[T]he actual number of neural connections going from the emotional centers to the cognitive centers is greater than the number going the other way. When an emotion is experienced it becomes a powerful motivator. . . affecting moment-to moment actions, attitudes and long-term achievements."

[Institute for HeartMath (1988), Boulder Creek, California, www.heartmath.org]

"We should take care not to make the intellect our god; it has powerful muscles, but no personality."

—Albert Einstein

". . . the amygdala projects back to the neo-cortex in a much stronger sense than the neo-cortex projects to the amygdala. . . . The implication is that the ability of the amygdala to control the cortex is greater than the ability of the cortex to control the amygdala. And this may explain why it's so hard for us to will away anxiety; emotions, once they're set into play, are very difficult to turn off."

[LeDoux, J. (1998). *The Emotional Brain: The Mysterious Underpinnings of Emotional Life*. New York: Touchstone]

"Although the limbic system theory is inadequate as an explanation of the specific brain circuits of emotion, MacLean's original ideas are insightful and quite interesting in the context of general evolutionary explanation of emotion and the brain. In particular, the notion that emotions involve relatively primitive circuits that are conserved throughout mammalian evolution seems right on target. Further, the argument that cognitive processes might involve other circuits, and might function relatively independent of emotional circuits, at least in some cases, also seems correct."

[LeDoux, J. (2002). *Synapatic Self: How Our Brains Become Who We Are*. New York: Penguin]

"The idea that emotions are inherently rational has a long history. Both Aristotle and Spinoza obviously thought that at least some emotions, in the right circumstances, were rational . . . The contemporary philosophers Ronald de Sousa and Martha Nussbaum also have argued persuasively for the rationality of emotion. In this context the term rational does not denote explicit logical reasoning but rather an association with actions or outcomes that are beneficial to the organism exhibiting emotions."

[Damasio, A. (2003). *Looking for Spinoza: Joy, Sorrow, and the Feeling Brain*. Orlando: Harcourt, Inc.]

FIGHT!! FIGHT!!

"Rats—better yet, frightened rats—are the key, says Dr. Joseph LeDoux, a 46-year-old neuroscientist at New York University who pioneered the study of emotions as biological phenomena . . .

"Anatomists like Dr. LeDoux 'are funny people,' said Dr. Paul MacLean, the scientist who coined the term limbic system. 'They think only about fear and rage,' said Dr. MacLean, a senior researcher at the National Institute of Mental Health's Neuroscience Center in Washington. 'They forget love, which more than anything else accounts for the development of the human race.'"

[Blakeslee, S., "Using Rats to Trace Anatomy of Fear, Biology of Emotion," *The New York Times*, November 5, 1996]

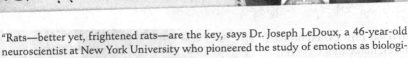

"I like to think of humans as rats with two legs."

—Dr. Craig Kinsey, researcher, in Carmichael, M., "Science: Mother Knows Best," *Newsweek*, November 17, 2003

```
32:45
32:24
30:45
34:13
34:20
35:50
34:58
39:42
36:49
93:35
99:49
47:23
34:16
 2:59
 3:20
= 9:53:10
```

"I HAVE THE HEART OF A CHILD. I KEEP IT IN A JAR ON MY SHELF."
— ROBERT BLOCH

What fresh hell is this?

– *Dorothy Parker*

HERE'S A REAL EXAMPLE OF LEADERSHIP
AS DEFINED BY THE ENTERPISE. ONLY 48
THINGS TO DO—PERFECTLY, SIMUTANEOUSLY,
CONSTANTLY, SELFLESSLY AND IN ADDITION
TO EVERYTHING ELSE— AND YOU'RE A LEADER.

OUR ENTERPRISE LEADERSHIP COMPETENCY MODEL

LEADS the Business

Drives Results
1. Exhibits a relentless drive to get things done by focusing on priority results over activity.
2. Sets and measures desired goals, tracking outcomes versus expected results in a fact-based manner.
3. Acts with a sense of urgency to meet deadlines and expectations.
4. Effectively allocates resources to projects that will deliver the most value.

Executes Business Strategy
1. Translates his or her vision into realistic business strategies.
2. Utilizes economic, industry and competitor trends and insights to drive business decisions.
3. Turns customer/client needs into desirable, profitable products and services.

Promotes Enterprise Culture
1. Makes decisions that optimize the results and performance of the whole organization, not just own business or function.
2. Offers talent, systems, best practices, technology and solutions to benefit the organization.
3. Encourages direct and open debate about important issues affecting the enterprise, even if beyond accountabilities.

Causes Change
1. Sets tone and direction by clearly articulating vision.
2. Enlists others to commit and drive meaningful change.
3. Finds practical ways to overcome barriers to change.

LEADS Others

Attracts Top Talent
1. Clearly determines evolving talent needs (type, skill set levels, quantities) as part of an ongoing business planning.
2. Establishes and maintains high recruiting standards to ensure "adds" to the organization are talent upgrades.
3. Proactively recruits for talent by maintaining networks, and doing opportunistic and creative hiring as appropriate.
4. Acquires high-caliber people with a diversity of skills and backgrounds.

Holds Others Accountable
1. Clarifies acceptable behavior and sets boundaries.
2. Provides honest, constructive feedback on achievements.
3. Aggressively manages underperformers, taking action in a timely manner consistent with company policy.

Creates and Sustains a Dynamic Workplace
1. Genuinely seeks and values others' unique talents and viewpoints.
2. Identifies and removes barriers to effective interactions with and across work groups.
3. Focuses on constructive problem solving vs. blame to encourage risk taking.
4. Obtains needed talent, resources and information to maximize organization's effectiveness.

Maximizes Individual and Organizational Performance
1. Delegates work that provides substantial responsibility and visibility.
2. Leverages what motivates an individual to perform at their best.
3. Arranges assignments, training and other experiences to develop capabilities strategic to the business and the individual.

Aligns Rewards
1. Uses the reward system to distinguish top performers and discourage underperformance.
2. Provides tangible rewards for significant performance.
3. Recognizes all factors of performance: business results and personal effectiveness.

LEADS Self

Exhibits Courage, Conviction and Credibility
1. Takes the lead on unpopular though necessary actions.
2. Acts decisively to tackle difficult problems.
3. Exhibits character through words and deeds, encourages honesty throughout the organization.
4. Is viewed as capable, effective and able to enlist others.

Applies Critical Thinking
1. Analyzes complex issues and problems, then synthesizes information to identify key issues and make decisions.
2. Focuses on the big picture in a complex situation and relies on guiding values and intuition to arrive at the best course of action.
3. Integrates different perspectives and ideas.

Demonstrates Self-Awareness
1. Demonstrates a strong drive to achieve with a balance of humility.
2. Seeks and embraces candid feedback with resiliency.
3. Reflects on and learns from experience.
4. Admits mistakes and faults.

Communicates Effectively and Influences Others
1. Clearly articulates even the most complex concepts so others understand.
2. Influences others without using formal authority.
3. Is open to being influenced to explore new possibilities.

> Here is Edward Bear, coming downstairs now, bump, bump, bump, on the back of his head ... It is, as far as he knows, the only way of coming downstairs, but sometimes he feels that there really is another way, if only he could stop bumping for a moment and think of it."
>
> **—A. A. Milne**

MARTIN LUTHER KING, JR.

HIS TOP VALUES

They sure seemed to be Equality, Freedom, Spirituality.

> "Revolutions are made by fanatical men of action with one-track minds, geniuses in their ability to confine themselves to a limited field."
> —Boris Pasternak

HIS BITTER PLACE

"There are those who are asking the devotees of civil rights, 'When will you be satisfied?' We can never be satisfied as long as our bodies, heavy with the fatigue of travel, cannot gain lodging in the motels of the highways and the hotels of the cities. We cannot be satisfied as long as the Negro's basic mobility is from a smaller ghetto to a larger one. We can never be satisfied as long as a Negro in Mississippi cannot vote and a Negro in New York believes he has nothing for which to vote."

HIS BETTER PLACE

"I say to you today, my friends, that in spite of the difficulties and frustrations of the moment, I still have a dream. It is a dream deeply rooted in the American dream. I have a dream that one day this nation will rise up and live out the true meaning of its creed: 'We hold these truths to be self-evident: that all men are created equal.' I have a dream that one day on the red hills of Georgia, the sons of former slaves and the sons of former slave owners will be able to sit down together at a table of brotherhood. I have a dream that one day even the state of Mississippi, a desert state, sweltering with the heat of injustice and oppression, will be transformed into an oasis of freedom and justice. I have a dream that my four children will one day live in a nation where they will not be judged by the color of their skin, but by the content of their character."

In 1994, the Ku Klux Klan applied to participate in Missouri's highway cleanup program and commit to regularly maintaining a stretch of Interstate 55, south of St. Louis. This would require the state to post signs proclaiming, "Next mile adopted by Knights of the Ku Klux Klan, Realm of Missouri."

The Missouri Department of Transportation refused their application, citing the federal Civil Rights Act, which prohibits funding of racial discrimination. The Klan sued the state and won. The U.S. Supreme Court awarded them the right to adopt the stretch of road.

The Missouri state legislature voted unanimously to rename that portion of Interstate 55 . . .

The Rosa Parks Highway.

> "Human salvation lies in the hands of the creatively maladjusted."
> —Martin Luther King, Jr.

Marcus Aurelius
David Ben-Gurion
Boudicca
Buddha
Mary Burt
Julius Caesar
Catherine the Great
Jesus Christ
Winston Churchill
Charles de Gaulle
Elizabeth I
Betty Friedan
Frederick II
Mohandas Gandhi
David Gorman
Hatshepsut
Janet Jagan
Thomas Jefferson

Martin Luther King, Jr.
Abraham Lincoln
Nelson Mandela
Wilma Mankiller
Karl Marx
Marlborough
George Marshall
Lorenzo de' Medici
Mohammed
Napoleon
Pericles
Ronald Reagan
Franklin D. Roosevelt
Theodore Roosevelt
Margaret Thatcher
Mother Teresa
George Washington
Wellington
Oprah Winfrey
Wu Zetian

NELSON MANDELA

HIS TOP VALUES
They sure seemed to be Equality, Freedom and Determination.

HIS BITTER PLACE
"The destruction caused by apartheid is incalculable. The fabric of family life of millions of my people has been shattered. Millions are homeless and unemployed. Our economy lies in ruins and our people are embroiled in political strife."

HIS BETTER PLACE
From his inaugural speech, May 10, 1994:
"Never, never and never again shall it be that this beautiful land will again experience the oppression of one by another and suffer the indignity of being the skunk of the world. We enter into a covenant that we shall build the society in which all South Africans, both black and white, will be able to walk tall, without any fear in their hearts, assured of their inalienable right to human dignity—a rainbow nation, at peace with itself and the world."

THREATENED BY HIS LEADERSHIP
Apartheid and all who supported it. All who were profiting from the large supply of cheap black labor. South Africa's National Party, which had been heavily backed for decades by the nation's trade unions and farmers—by far the biggest advocates of continuing apartheid.

"NDAPITA KU MALIRO."
—AFRICAN NYAU FOR
"I AM GOING TO THE FUNERAL,
LOCK UP THE CHICKEN."

"NILIKUUONYESHA NYOTA NA ULIANGALIA KIDOLE TU."
(SWAHILI FOR "I POINTED OUT THE STARS TO YOU AND ALL YOU SAW WAS THE TIP OF MY FINGER.")

AGNES GONXHA BOJAHIU
DBA MOTHER TERESA

HER TOP VALUES
They sure seemed to be Compassion, Spirituality and Service.

HER BITTER PLACE
"We the unwilling, led by the unknowing, are doing the impossible for the ungrateful. We have done so much, for so long, with so little, we are now qualified to do anything with nothing."

HER BETTER PLACE
"We see the poor people, we see the young people that are diseased, unwanted, unloved, a throwaway of society. Are we there? To be that love, that kindness, that thoughtfulness to them? And share the pain, the terrible pain, the terrible feeling of terrible loneliness. Be a throwaway. Have no one to be somebody to somebody."

At the time of her death, Mother Teresa's Missionaries of Charity had over 4,000 sisters, an associated brotherhood of 300 members, operating 610 missions in 123 countries.

> *I know God will not give me anything I can't handle. I just wish that He didn't trust me so much.*
> —Mother Teresa

LALA LAJPAT RAI SARANI
AJC BOSE ROAD, KOLKATA
700020 003 2227 8176

323-299-2447

(86) 571 8780-8292

"The study of monkeys also supports the idea that being a leader may greatly reinforce the qualities required to be effective. Work by Michael McGuire, a neuroscientist, formerly at the University of California, Los Angeles, found that high-ranking monkeys had high levels of serotonin, a compound that produces a sense of calm, well-being and self-confidence. But the high level appeared to be the consequence, not the cause, of high rank.

[Denning, Paul, "Creating Leaders," *The Economist*, October 2003]

"I personally think we developed language because of our deep inner need to complain."
—Jane Wagner

"Experiments with vervet monkey troops have discovered that subordinate males invariably have much lower serotonin levels than the alpha male. But when the alpha is removed from the group, the winner of the dominance contest to succeed him immediately inherits his elevated serotonin level . . . (McGuire, Raleigh and Brammer, 1984)."

["Dominance Seeking: A Neglected Criminogenic Trait," unpublished paper by Mike Wahn, associate professor, University of Winnipeg]

Monkeys are superior to men in this: when a monkey looks into a mirror, he sees a monkey.
—Malcolm de Chazal

"The remarkable social complexity of primates is brought about by their capacity to a) alter competitive outcomes and dominance positions through collaboration, and b) establish interindividual relationships for this very reason. Alliance formation links the vertical and horizontal components of social organization by making the individual's dominance position dependent on its place in the affiliative network. Consequently, this network becomes an arena of dominance-related strategy."

[De Waal, F. and Tyack, P., editors (2005). *Animal Social Complexity: Intelligence, Culture and Individualized Societies.* Cambridge: Harvard University Press]

Singapore 200

ADMIT ONE ADULT
PARK OPENS AT 7PM

NIGHT SAFARI

"I've actually gone to the zoo and had monkeys shout to me from their cages, 'I'm in here when you're walking around like that?'"

—Robin Williams

1

Abraham Maslow first introduced the hierarchy of needs in a 1943 paper entitled "A Theory of Human Motivation." It was embraced enthusiastically, almost without skepticism, which made Maslow skeptical. According to a paper published by the University of Alberta in Canada and other sources, he wrote in his personal journal in 1962 that "My motivation theory was published 20 years ago and in all that time nobody repeated it or tested it or really analyzed it or criticized it. They just used it, swallowed it whole with only the most minor modifications."

So he set about doing the tweaking himself, including slicing some of the hierarchy categories into multiple drivers. The consideration most applicable to your leadership is that self-actualization includes not only ultimate fulfillment of the self but selflessness, which he termed "self-transcendence" and described as "the connection to something beyond the ego and to help others find fulfillment." Living your own values and ultimately helping people to better live theirs will move you toward this highest level.

Most of his considered revisions were confined to his private writings and none of them have impacted the overwhelming acceptance of the original theory. The biggest pushback comes from multiple subsequent studies contradicting his assertion that needs must be met individually; it is believed that people are able to hold and satisfy multiple needs simultaneously.

2

"We argue that transcendence can best be thought of as an acceptance of something greater than the self. Out of this acceptance comes an understanding of the small role that one plays in a vast universe, an appreciation of others, and a recognition that others have a positive worth. Transcendence brings about having a proper perspective on life."

[Morris, J. A., Brotheridge, C. M. and Urbanski, J. C. (2005). "Bringing Humility to Leadership: Antecedents and Consequences of Leader Humility." *Human Relations* 10, pp. 1323–1350]

3

Maslow wasn't the first to consider motivations in a hierarchical format. William James, a pretty pragmatic guy and a founding father of psychology, was thinking that way many decades earlier and had also theorized that there are three levels of human needs: material (physiological, safety), social (belonging and self-actualization), and spiritual. And he wasn't the last: Allport (1960), Alderfer (1972) and Mathes (1981) theorized credible if slightly different concepts.

While there doesn't seem to be a lot of disagreement about what the concept of basic human needs is, there's heated competition to claim the biggest number of them. Nobria, Lawrence and Wilson (2001) say that there are four basic needs, so eat that, Maslow. The Institute for Management Excellence (2001) says that there are nine basic human needs, so wait in the car, Nobria, Lawrence and Wilson. In 1998, Ohio State University psychology professor Steven Reiss developed something called the "Reissprofile" (see: Maslow and the need for significance), claiming that there are sixteen basic needs, or what he termed "basic desires." Not to be outdone, Barneys department store in New York stocks 4,371 of what they term "basic desires."

Your strategies may be rocket science. Perfect. We're in the ro— —ce busin

et fuel business. (SM)

—ience. Perfect. We're in

The bad news is that there is no key to the universe.
The good news is that it was never locked.

—Swami Beyondananda

FROM MASLOW, THE GUY YOU WANT TO STUDY FOR HIS THEORIES ON HUMAN MOTIVATION AS IT APPLIES TO INCENTIVIZING PEOPLE TO SUPPORT YOUR DEEPEST PERSONAL VALUES:

- "Behavior in the human being is sometimes a defense, a way of concealing motives and thoughts."

- "What conditions of work, what kinds of work, what kinds of management, and what kinds of reward or pay will help human stature to grow healthy, to its fuller and fullest stature? Classic economic theory, based as it is on an inadequate theory of human motivation, could be revolutionized by accepting the reality of higher human needs, including the impulse to self-actualization and the love for the highest values."

- "The story of the human race is the story of men and women selling themselves short."

- "The key question isn't 'What fosters creativity?' But it is why in God's name isn't everyone creative? Where was the human potential lost? How was it crippled? I think therefore a good question might be not why do people create? But why do people not create or innovate? We have got to abandon that sense of amazement in the face of creativity, as if it were a miracle if anybody created anything."

- "If you plan on being anything less than you are capable of being, you will probably be unhappy all the days of your life."

FROM MASLOW, THE GUY YOU WANT TO HOIST A BUNCH OF BEERS WITH:

- "EVERY REALLY NEW IDEA LOOKS CRAZY AT FIRST."

- "IF THE ONLY TOOL YOU HAVE IS A HAMMER IT'S TEMPTING TO TREAT EVERYTHING AS A NAIL."

- "A FIRST-RATE SOUP IS MORE CREATIVE THAN A SECOND-RATE PAINTING."

- "IF YOU TREAT YOUR CHILDREN AT HOME IN THE SAME WAY YOU TREAT YOUR ANIMALS IN THE LAB, YOUR WIFE WILL SCRATCH YOUR EYES OUT."

- "I WAS AWFULLY CURIOUS TO FIND OUT WHY I DIDN'T GO INSANE."

ect. We're in the rocket fuel bus

Uhl-Bien, Marion and McKelvey claim that the leadership models of the twentieth century are outdated for the organizational requirements of the twenty-first, which are a lot more complex and require contributions and input from all levels. "Formal leaders" have to prepare for a new approach because we're in what they call a knowledge era, vs. a production era, and old models of leading just don't work. Check out their thinking at:

Uhl-Bien, M., Marion, R. and McKelvey, B. (2007). "Complexity Leadership Theory: Shifting Leadership from the Industrial Age to the Knowledge Era," *The Leadership Quarterly* 18, pp. 298–318.

"I got some new underwear last week. Well, new to me."
—Emo Philips

Your strategies may be rocket scie

"One of the foundations of emotional competence—accurate self assessment—was associated with superior performance among several hundred managers from 12 different organizations."

[Source: Richard Boyatzis (1982) The Competent Manager: A Model for Effective Performance. New York: John Wiley and Sons]

Mitchie & Gootie (2005) offer a positive perspective on the role of emotions in leadership and authenticity. They address the following questions: What role do values (thoughts) and emotions (feelings) play in distinguishing between authentic and inauthentic leaders? (Mitchie, S. & Gootie, J. (2005), "Values, Emotions, and Authenticity: Will the Real Leader Please Stand Up?" *The Leadership Quarterly* 16 (3), pp. 441–457).

"What's shakin', chiefy baby?"

(Thurgood Marshall's customary greeting to Chief Justice Warren E. Burger)

2:46 AM 1/3/06
HUNTING THE ELUSIVE ADVERB

Engagement at work was conceptualized by Kahn (1990) as the "harnessing of organizational members' selves to their work roles; in engagement, people employ and express themselves physically, cognitively, and emotionally during role performances' (p. 694). For Kahn, self and role "exist in some dynamic, negotiable relation in which a person both drives personal energies into role behaviors (self-employment) and displays the self within the role (self-expression)" (p. 700). Such engagement serves to fulfill the human spirit at work.

Alternatively, disengagement is viewed as the decoupling of the self from the work role and involves people withdrawing and defending themselves during role performances. Such 'unemployment' of the self in one's role is considered robotic or apathetic behavior. (Hochschild, 1983).

. . . "Individuals who believe that a given work role activity is personally meaningful are likely to be motivated to invest themselves more fully in it. Indeed, previous research in the job design area has demonstrated that meaningfulness is linked with internal work motivation. (Fried & Ferris, 1987; Renn & Vandenberg, 1995)."

[May, D. R., Gilson, R. L., Harter L. M. (2004). "The Psychological Conditions of Meaningfulness, Safety and Availability and the Engagement of the Human Spirit at Work." *Journal of Occupational and Organizational Psychology* 77, pp.11–37]

"WE ARE HAPPY WHEN FOR EVERYTHING INSIDE US THERE IS A CORRESPONDING SOMETHING OUTSIDE US."

—YEATS

"Nascent research on authentic leadership is clearly relevant to the topic of hypocrisy. Leaders who are authentic know who they are, what they believe and value, and act upon those values and beliefs while transparently interacting with others. (Avolio, Gardner, Walumbwa, Luthans, & May, 2004, p. 803)."

[Cha, S. E. and Edmondson, A. C. (2006). "When Values Backfire: Leadership, Attribution and Disenchantment in a Values-Driven Organization," *The Leadership Quarterly* 17, pp. 57–78]

"Sometimes when I'm smiling and shaking hands, I want to kick them."
—Richard Nixon

"In the absence of psychological safety, leaders who become seen as hypocritical may be the last to know. Leaders must work particularly hard to make their own actions discussable through frequent invitations for feedback, inquiry into what others are thinking and feeling, and expressions of vulnerability that make it possible to express concerns and questions. (Argyris, 1993; Edmondson, Roberto, & Watkins, 2003)."

[Cha, S. E. and Edmondson, A. C. (2006). "When Values Backfire: Leadership, Attribution and Disenchantment in a Values-Driven Organization," *The Leadership Quarterly* 17, pp. 57–78]

The bravest act of a warrior is to allow someone
to reach past his armor to touch his heart.

"In the 21st century, managing must include two perspectives:

- "The unlearning of deeply ingrained, self-limiting assumptions about
  individualism, authority and responsibility that defeat cooperation and
  paradoxically, individual success.

- "Looking outward toward the wider social and business networks that
  shape their mutual effort. People need both relationship and environment
  perspectives to make sense of the workplace."

[Weisborg, M. R. (2004). *Productive Workplaces Revisited*. San Francisco, CA:
Jossey-Bass]

We must be our own before we can be another's. —Emerson

"Authentic behavior can be distinguished from inauthentic behavior by the conscious,
motivated intentions that underlie it. Authentic behavior involves an honest assessment
of one's self-aspects via awareness and unbiased processing components. In essence,
authentic behavior implies choice and is motivated to solve self-relevant problems. In turn,
inauthentic behavior involves being unaware of, ignoring, oversimplifying, and/or distorting
self-aspects relevant to the behavioral context."

[Kernis, M. and Goldman, M.: *Authenticity, Consciousness and Social Motivation* also Goldman, M.H. "The Role of
Authenticity in Optimal Psychological Functioning and Subjective Well-being." *Annals of Psychotherapy* also Kernis,
M.H. (in press). "Toward a Conceptualization of Optimal Self-esteem." *Psychological Inquiry*]

"Leaders who are high on emotional intelligence may instill in their
organizations a sense of enthusiasm, excitement, and optimism as well as
an atmosphere of cooperation and trust through their being able to develop
high quality interpersonal relationships with their followers. High quality
interpersonal relationships between leaders and their followers have been
documented to produce numerous advantages for organizations, leaders,
and followers. (Gerstner & Day, 1997; Graen & Uhl-Bien, 1995)"

[George, J. (2005). "Leadership Emotions and Leadership: The Role of Emotional
Intelligence," Part 8 in I. Nonaka (ed), *Critical Perspectives on Business and
Management*. New York: Routledge]

"In the end, great organizations know that a reason-driven economy can travel only
so far. The missing link is the engagement of deep-seated emotions as the driver
of growth and profits. These—and only these—feelings are the fuel that propels
talented individuals to do more, and inspire customers to return.

[Curt W. Coffman and Gabriel Gonzales-Molina (2002). *How the World's Greatest Organizations Drive
Growth by Unleashing Human Potential*. New York: Warner Books]

"NO EXCELLENT SOUL IS EXEMPT FROM A MIXTURE OF MADNESS."
—ARISTOTLE

"EVERYTHING HAS BEEN FIGURED OUT
EXCEPT HOW TO LIVE."
—JEAN-PAUL SARTE

"For 515 senior executives analyzed by the search firm Egon Zehnder International, those who were primarily strong in emotional intelligence were more likely to succeed than those who were strongest in either relevant previous experience or IQ. More specifically, the executive was high in emotional intelligence in 74 percent of the successes and only in 24 percent of the failures. The study included executives in Latin America, Germany, and Japan, and the results were almost identical in all three cultures.

[Geist, Sam (2001). *Would You Work for You?*. Toronto: Addington and Wentworth]

"Only 51 percent of senior managers and 21 percent of middle managers have personal values linked with strategy."

[Kaplan, R. S. and Norton, D. P. (2001). *The Strategy-Focused Organization*. Boston: Harvard Business School Press]

"Before I got into rock and roll, I was going to be a dentist."
—*Gregg Allman*

"We have shown that animals exposed to continuous stress for long periods of time go through three phases of adaptability: the initial alarm reaction, followed by resistance, and eventually exhaustion."

[Sele, Hans (1974). *Stress without Distress*. New York: J.B. Lippincott]

"The antidote to exhaustion is not necessarily rest. The antidote to exhaustion is wholeheartedness."
—*Brother David Steindl-Rast*

"Let the beauty of what you love be what you do."
—*Rumi*

"Now come on take a walk with me, Arlene, and tell me who do you love?"
—BO DIDDLEY

"BO DIDDLEY WAS SO SEXY THAT HE TOLD ARLENE HE HAD A CHIMNEY MADE OF HUMAN SKULLS — AND SHE STILL WENT FOR A WALK WITH HIM."
—TODD SNIDER

I wish you fair skies and a tight grip.

—*E. B. White*